Laravel 5 Essentials

Explore the fundamentals of Laravel, one of the most expressive and robust PHP frameworks available

Martin Bean

[PACKT]
PUBLISHING

BIRMINGHAM - MUMBAI

Laravel 5 Essentials

Copyright © 2015 Packt Publishing

First published: April 2015

Production reference: 1240415

Published by Packt Publishing Ltd.
Livery Place
35 Livery Street
Birmingham B3 2PB, UK.

ISBN 978-1-78528-301-7

www.packtpub.com

Credits

Author
Martin Bean

Reviewers
Si Fleming
Michael Peacock
Brayan Laurindo Rastelli
Michele Somma

Commissioning Editor
Akram Hussain

Acquisition Editor
Reshma Raman

Content Development Editor
Mohammed Fahad

Technical Editor
Ankur Ghiye

Copy Editors
Merilyn Pereira
Laxmi Subramanian

Project Coordinator
Danuta Jones

Proofreaders
Safis Editing
Paul Hindle

Indexer
Monica Ajmera Mehta

Production Coordinator
Nilesh R. Mohite

Cover Work
Nilesh R. Mohite

About the Author

Martin Bean is a full-stack website developer based in Newcastle upon Tyne, UK. Prior to writing this book, he spent 8 years as a professional website developer, beginning his career and honing his skills in various agencies. After 5 years, he made the switch to running his own development and consultancy firm, where he worked with clients, both big and small.

Although this is the first book he has authored, he has written other articles and acted as a technical reviewer on a Node.js title. He also blogs regularly on his own website, `http://martinbean.co.uk`.

You can follow Martin on Twitter at `https://twitter.com/martinbean`.

I would like to thank the team at Packt Publishing for reaching out and giving me the opportunity to author this book. It's truly an honor to be recognized and asked to write this book. I'd also like to thank my girlfriend, Vikki, who was surprisingly calm when I told her I was taking time away from work to write this book, and who also plied me with dozens of cups of tea throughout the writing process. A note of thanks also goes out to the editors and reviewers of this title to ensure it is of the highest quality, and a final thank you goes to you, the reader, for purchasing this book and making the many hours I put into this book worth it.

About the Reviewers

Si Fleming is a senior engineer with experience in working with Java and PHP for over a decade. He holds a PhD in computer science from the University of Sussex, where his research focused on distributed systems, ad hoc social networks, Q&A, security, and privacy.

Michael Peacock is an experienced software developer and team lead from Newcastle, UK, with a degree in software engineering from the University of Durham.

After spending a number of years running his own web agency and subsequently working directly for a number of software start-ups, Michael now runs his own software development agency, working on a range of projects for an array of different clients.

He is the author of *Creating Development Environments with Vagrant*, *PHP 5 Social Networking*, *PHP 5 E-Commerce Development*, *Drupal 7 Social Networking*, *Selling Online with Drupal e-Commerce*, and *Building Websites with TYPO3*, all by *Packt Publishing*. The other publications Michael has been involved in include *Advanced API Security*, *Mobile Web Development*, *Jenkins Continuous Integration Cookbook*, and *Drupal for Education and E-Learning*, for which he acted as a technical reviewer.

Michael has also presented at a number of user groups and technical conferences, including PHP UK Conference, Dutch PHP Conference, ConFoo, PHPNE, PHPNW, and CloudConnect Santa Clara.

You can follow Michael on Twitter at @michaelpeacock or find out more about him through his website at www.michaelpeacock.co.uk.

Brayan Laurindo Rastelli has been involved in web development for more than 6 years now and is always in pursuit of new and cool technologies to work with. Brayan has a passion for making things faster and more efficient. He carries with him an extensive knowledge of PHP, most notably the Laravel framework, having created a Laravel course to train Brazilians. In addition, Brayan has also created and maintained both the website and forum for the Laravel community in Brazil. Currently, he works at Speed to Contact on a single page/real-time application using Laravel, AngularJS, WebSockets, telephony, and other cutting-edge technologies.

Michael Somma is an Italian web developer skilled in PHP, MySQL, and some new frameworks such as jQuery, jQuery UI, and Twitter Bootstrap. For over 2 years, he has been a major user of the PHP CodeIgniter framework and has now migrated to the Laravel framework. He likes to develop both application frontend and backend with new technology that learns. Since 2010, he has worked at a web agency in Bari (Italy), developing a large variety of websites and web applications; in 2014, he started his own activity. As part of Github, he tries to contribute to various projects in his spare time.

www.PacktPub.com

Support files, eBooks, discount offers, and more

For support files and downloads related to your book, please visit www.PacktPub.com.

Did you know that Packt offers eBook versions of every book published, with PDF and ePub files available? You can upgrade to the eBook version at www.PacktPub.com and as a print book customer, you are entitled to a discount on the eBook copy. Get in touch with us at service@packtpub.com for more details.

At www.PacktPub.com, you can also read a collection of free technical articles, sign up for a range of free newsletters and receive exclusive discounts and offers on Packt books and eBooks.

https://www2.packtpub.com/books/subscription/packtlib

Do you need instant solutions to your IT questions? PacktLib is Packt's online digital book library. Here, you can search, access, and read Packt's entire library of books.

Why subscribe?

- Fully searchable across every book published by Packt
- Copy and paste, print, and bookmark content
- On demand and accessible via a web browser

Free access for Packt account holders

If you have an account with Packt at www.PacktPub.com, you can use this to access PacktLib today and view 9 entirely free books. Simply use your login credentials for immediate access.

Table of Contents

Preface

Application frameworks have grown in popularity over the past five years. There has been a tremendous shift from handwriting all code to leveraging these powerful frameworks with prebuilt components and features. However, with anything that comes to be in fashion, there are now a lot of contending options, and each of them viable.

While CodeIgniter was one of the first frameworks to enjoy widespread popularity, this popularity would come to be its undoing years later, as its large spread use and low barrier to entry meant it couldn't take advantage of newer versions of PHP without losing backwards compatibility, and potentially breaking lots of applications. This saw it then be surpassed by faster-moving alternatives such as Symfony and even FuelPHP, which was developed as a response to CodeIgniter's unwillingness to embrace change.

Enter: Laravel. Laravel joined the framework scene when there were already many players. However, the developers of Laravel used this timing to their advantage, instead creating a framework that avoided all of the problems and mistakes previous full stack frameworks had made and building on top of the excellent Symfony components in order to create a robust, component-based framework.

Instead of providing dozens of inflexible libraries, Laravel provides sensible, driver-based components that developers could use to build applications their own way, rather than trying to mash everything into the layout the framework author defined. This led to Laravel rising in popularity. It was also a fast-moving framework, and, by version 4, had become the most starred framework on GitHub, a testament to its popularity.

This book will give you a tour of Laravel and its core features. We'll look at how to manage multiple Laravel applications on the same machine and then we'll go ahead and start building our own Laravel application from scratch through to completion. Once we've got a basic application reading and writing data from a database, we'll take a look at Eloquent, Laravel's ORM, which is what makes it easy to read and write from a database and the more advanced features it offers. From there, we'll look at Artisan, Laravel's command-line utility, and even how to define our own commands. We'll then learn how to write automated tests for our application to make sure it keeps working the way we want it to, even with future developments. Then, finally, we'll look at how to build login and registration systems using Laravel's user authentication component.

By the end of the book, you'll have a complete Laravel application, as well as the tools and knowledge of how to build your own Laravel-based applications unassisted, and where to continue your learning of the framework.

What this book covers

Chapter 1, An Introduction to Laravel, takes a look at application frameworks in PHP in general, a recent history of the Laravel framework, and the principles that the Laravel framework is built upon.

Chapter 2, Setting Up a Development Environment, lays the foundation for what's needed to build Laravel applications by installing and configuring the Homestead virtual machine and the Composer dependency manager.

Chapter 3, Your First Application, builds a working application in Laravel from start to finish. Here is where the fun begins!

Chapter 4, Eloquent ORM, takes a look at Eloquent, the object relation mapper that ships with Laravel and allows you to query your databases easily.

Chapter 5, Testing – It's Easier Than You Think, goes over the various approaches to test your Laravel applications to make sure they're as solid as possible and still work as intended after adding new features.

Chapter 6, A Command-line Companion Called Artisan, helps us meet Artisan, the command-line utility for Laravel. We cover the commands Artisan offers out of the box, as well as how to create our own command-line tools.

Chapter 7, Authentication and Security, shows you the various ways to protect your Laravel applications from common attacks, as well as how to authenticate and authorize users accessing your application.

Appendix, An Arsenal of Tools, covers the arsenal of tools that Laravel provides, which haven't been covered in the previous chapters.

What you need for this book

As Laravel is a PHP-based application framework, you will need a code editor or IDE with syntax highlighting for PHP.

We'll be using the Homestead virtual machine, which requires both Vagrant and VirtualBox to be installed on your machine; installation instructions for both of these will be provided later in the book.

Also, if you plan to deploy applications to a live web server, then you will need an FTP client or SSH access to the remote web server in order to move the files from your local machine to the web-accessible server.

Who this book is for

This book is primarily aimed at those interested in learning about the Laravel framework, as maybe they've heard about it but not had the chance or time to become familiar with it. Therefore, knowledge of PHP and related technologies (such as MySQL) is assumed, as is knowledge of object-oriented programming.

Conventions

In this book, you will find a number of text styles that distinguish between different kinds of information. Here are some examples of these styles and an explanation of their meaning.

Code words in text, database table names, folder names, filenames, file extensions, pathnames, dummy URLs, user input, and Twitter handles are shown as follows: "The Illuminate namespace does not refer to a third-party library."

A block of code is set as follows:

```
sites:
    - map: dev.furbook.com
      to: /home/vagrant/Code/furbook.com/public
databases:
    - furbook
```

When we wish to draw your attention to a particular part of a code block, the relevant lines or items are set in bold:

```
Route::post('cats', function() {
  $cat = Furbook\Cat::create(Input::all());
  return redirect('cats/'.$cat->id)
    ->withSuccess('Cat has been created.');
});
```

Any command-line input or output is written as follows:

```
$ composer create-project laravel/laravel furbook.com --prefer-dist
```

New terms and **important words** are shown in bold. Words that you see on the screen, for example, in menus or dialog boxes, appear in the text like this: " If you now try to visit an invalid URL, nginx will display a **404 Not Found** error page."

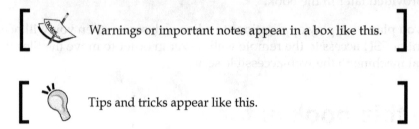

[Warnings or important notes appear in a box like this.]

[Tips and tricks appear like this.]

Reader feedback

Feedback from our readers is always welcome. Let us know what you think about this book—what you liked or disliked. Reader feedback is important for us as it helps us develop titles that you will really get the most out of.

To send us general feedback, simply e-mail feedback@packtpub.com, and mention the book's title in the subject of your message.

If there is a topic that you have expertise in and you are interested in either writing or contributing to a book, see our author guide at www.packtpub.com/authors.

Customer support

Now that you are the proud owner of a Packt book, we have a number of things to help you to get the most from your purchase.

Downloading the example code

You can download the example code files from your account at http://www.packtpub.com for all the Packt Publishing books you have purchased. If you purchased this book elsewhere, you can visit http://www.packtpub.com/support and register to have the files e-mailed directly to you.

Errata

Although we have taken every care to ensure the accuracy of our content, mistakes do happen. If you find a mistake in one of our books—maybe a mistake in the text or the code—we would be grateful if you could report this to us. By doing so, you can save other readers from frustration and help us improve subsequent versions of this book. If you find any errata, please report them by visiting http://www.packtpub.com/submit-errata, selecting your book, clicking on the **Errata Submission Form** link, and entering the details of your errata. Once your errata are verified, your submission will be accepted and the errata will be uploaded to our website or added to any list of existing errata under the Errata section of that title.

To view the previously submitted errata, go to https://www.packtpub.com/books/content/support and enter the name of the book in the search field. The required information will appear under the **Errata** section.

Piracy

Piracy of copyrighted material on the Internet is an ongoing problem across all media. At Packt, we take the protection of our copyright and licenses very seriously. If you come across any illegal copies of our works in any form on the Internet, please provide us with the location address or website name immediately so that we can pursue a remedy.

Please contact us at copyright@packtpub.com with a link to the suspected pirated material.

We appreciate your help in protecting our authors and our ability to bring you valuable content.

Questions

If you have a problem with any aspect of this book, you can contact us at questions@packtpub.com, and we will do our best to address the problem.

1
An Introduction to Laravel

PHP frameworks aren't new, but one of the newest on the block is Laravel. Since version 3, Laravel has exploded in popularity to become one of the most popular and widely used PHP frameworks in a short span of time. At the time of writing, the Laravel repository on GitHub has more stars than its more mature contemporaries such as Symfony, CakePHP, CodeIgniter, and Yii. So what is it about Laravel that makes it so popular?

In this chapter, we will cover the following topics:

- How the productivity can be increased using a framework
- The fundamental concepts and key features of Laravel
- The general structure and conventions of a new Laravel application
- An introduction to the Model-View-Controller (MVC) design pattern, on which Laravel is based
- Migration tips for users of the previous versions of Laravel

We will look at its key features and how they have made Laravel an indispensable tool for many web developers. We will compare writing PHP applications with and without a framework, and see how using a framework can aid in writing more robust and better-structured PHP applications. Then, we will take a closer look at the anatomy of a Laravel application and the third-party packages that it leverages. After reading this chapter, you will have the knowledge needed to get started and build your first Laravel application.

The need for frameworks

Of all the server-side programming languages, PHP undoubtedly has the lowest entry barriers. It is almost always installed by default on even the cheapest web hosts, and it is also extremely easy to set up on any personal computer. For newcomers who have some experience with authoring web pages in HTML and CSS, the concepts of variables, inline conditions, and `include` statements are easy to grasp. PHP also provides many commonly used functions that one might need when developing a dynamic website. All of this contributes to what some refer to as the **immediacy** of PHP. However, this instant gratification comes at a cost. It gives a false sense of productivity to beginners, who almost inevitably end up with convoluted spaghetti code as they add more features and functionality to their site. This is mainly because PHP, out of the box, does not do much to encourage the separation of concerns.

The limitations of homemade tools

If you already have a few PHP projects under your belt, but have not used a web application framework before, then you will probably have amassed a personal collection of commonly used functions and classes that you can use on new projects. These homegrown utilities might help you with common tasks, such as sanitizing data, authenticating users, and including pages dynamically. You might also have a predefined directory structure where these classes and the rest of your application code reside. However, all of this will exist in complete isolation; you will be solely responsible for the maintenance, inclusion of new features, and documentation. For a lone developer or an agency with ever-changing staff, this can be a tedious and time-consuming task, not to mention that if you were to collaborate with other developers on the project, they would first have to get acquainted with the way in which you build applications.

Laravel to the rescue

This is exactly where a web application framework such as Laravel comes to the rescue. Laravel reuses and assembles existing components to provide you with a cohesive layer upon which you can build your web applications in a more structured and pragmatic way. Drawing inspiration from popular frameworks written not just in PHP but other programming languages too, Laravel offers a robust set of tools and an application architecture that incorporates many of the best features of frameworks like CodeIgniter, Yii, ASP.NET MVC, Ruby on Rails, Sinatra, and others.

Most of these frameworks use the **Model-View-Controller (MVC)** paradigm or design pattern. If you have used one of the aforementioned tools or the MVC pattern, then you will find it quite easy to get started with Laravel 5.

A new approach to developing PHP applications

As previously mentioned, PHP gained a bad reputation over the years due to lots of badly-written websites and web applications, and its shortcomings when compared to other, more mature languages. PHP is also notorious for its naming inconsistencies and questionable design decisions regarding its syntax. As a consequence, there has been an exodus to more credible frameworks written in **Ruby** and **Python**. Since these languages were nowhere as feature-rich for the Web as PHP, the creators of Ruby on Rails and Django, for instance, had to recreate some essential building blocks, such as classes, to represent HTTP requests and responses and were, therefore, able to avoid some of the mistakes that PHP had made before them, due to the luxury of starting from a blank slate. These frameworks also forced the developer to adhere to a predefined application architecture.

However, it's now a great time to discover (or fall back in love with) PHP again, as over the past couple of years the language has rapidly evolved to include new features such as closures and traits, and a de facto package manager in Composer. Past complaints of PHP when compared to other languages are now exactly that, of the past, and PHP is slowly but surely changing the bad reputation it has suffered from, for so long.

A more robust HTTP foundation

After years of people developing their own, unique approach of handling common tasks, such as handling requests and responses, specifically for their own projects, one framework took a different approach and instead, began creating components that could be used in any codebase no matter its foundation, be it homegrown or based on a framework. The **Symfony** project adopted these principles to recreate a more solid, flexible, and testable HTTP foundation for PHP applications. Along with the latest version of Drupal and phpBB, Laravel is one of the many open source projects that use this foundation together with several other components that form the Symfony framework.

Laravel is such a project that relies on the HTTP foundation created by Symfony. It also relies on other components created by Symfony, as well as a variety of other popular libraries, such as **SwiftMailer** for more straightforward e-mailing, **Carbon** for more expressive date and time handling, **Doctrine** for its inflector and database abstraction tools, and a handful of other tools to handle logging, class loading, and error reporting. Instead of re-inventing the wheel, Laravel decided to hop on the shoulder of giants and embrace these pre-existing mature components.

Embracing PHP

One way in which Laravel differs from its contemporaries is that it openly embraces new features of PHP and in turn requires a fairly recent version (at least 5.4). Previously, other frameworks would build support for older versions of PHP to maintain backwards-compatibility for as long as possible. However, this approach meant that those same frameworks couldn't take advantage of new features in the newer versions of PHP, in turn, hampering the evolution of PHP. Using Laravel 5, you will get to grips with some of the newer features of PHP. If you're new to PHP, or coming back to the language after a while, then here's what you can expect to find:

- **Namespaces**: More mature languages such as Java and C# have namespaces. Namespaces help developers avoid naming collisions that might happen if say, two different libraries have the same function or class name. In PHP, namespaces are separated by backslashes, which is usually mirrored by the directory structure, with the only difference being the use of slashes on Unix systems, in accordance with the PSR-4 convention. A namespace, such as `<?php namespace Illuminate\Database\Eloquent` is declared at the top of the file. To use code from another namespace, it needs to be imported, which can be done with the `use` keyword, and then by specifying the namespace, that is, `use Illuminate\Database\Eloquent\Model`. Another advantage of namespaces is that you can alias imported classes, so as to avoid collisions with classes with the same name in another namespace or the global namespace. To do this, you use the `as` keyword after the `use` statement as `use Foo\Logger as FooLogger;`

- **Interfaces**: Interfaces specify the methods that a class should provide when that interface is implemented. Interfaces do not contain any implementation details themselves, merely the methods (and the arguments those methods should take). For instance, if a class implements Laravel's `JsonableInterface` instance, then that class will also need to have a `toJson()` method. Within Laravel, interfaces tend to be referred to as **Contracts**.

- **Anonymous functions**: These are also known as `closures` and were introduced in PHP 5.3. Somewhat reminiscent of JavaScript, they help you to produce shorter code, and you will use them extensively when building Laravel applications to define routes, events, filters, and in many other instances. This is an example of an anonymous function attached to a route: `Route::get('/', function() { return 'Hello, world.'; });`.In Laravel, this code creates a new **route** when the base path of a website is requested. When it is, the code in the closure is executed and returned as the response.

- **Overloading**: Also called `dynamic` methods, they allow you to call methods such as `whereUsernameOrEmail($name, $email)` that were not explicitly defined in a class. These calls get handled by the `__call()` method in the class, which then tries to parse the name to execute one or more known methods. In this case, `->where('username', $username)->orWhere('email', $email)`.

- **Shorter array syntax**: PHP 5.4 introduced the shorter array syntax. Instead of writing `array('primes' =>array(1,3,5,7))`, it is now possible to use just square brackets to denote an array, that is, `['primes'=>[1,3,5,7]]`. You might know syntax if you've used arrays in JavaScript.

Laravel's main features and sources of inspiration

So, what do you get out of the box with Laravel 5? Let's take a look and see how the following features can help boost your productivity:

- **Modularity**: Laravel was built on top of over 20 different libraries and is itself split into individual modules. Tightly integrated with **Composer** dependency manager, these components can be updated with ease.

- **Testability**: Built from the ground up to ease testing, Laravel ships with several helpers that let you visit routes from your tests, crawl the resulting HTML, ensure that methods are called on certain classes, and even impersonate authenticated users in order to make sure the right code is run at the right time.

- **Routing**: Laravel gives you a lot of flexibility when you define the routes of your application. For example, you could manually bind a simple anonymous function to a route with an HTTP verb, such as GET, POST, PUT, or DELETE. This feature is inspired by micro-frameworks, such as **Sinatra** (Ruby) and **Silex** (PHP).

- **Configuration management**: More often than not, your application will be running in different environments, which means that the database or e-mail server credential's settings or the displaying of error messages will be different when your app is running on a local development server to when it is running on a production server. Laravel has a consistent approach to handle configuration settings, and different settings can be applied in different environments via the use of an `.env` file, containing settings unique for that environment.

- **Query builder and ORM**: Laravel ships with a fluent query builder, which lets you issue database queries with a PHP syntax, where you simply chain methods instead of writing SQL. In addition to this, it provides you with an **Object Relational Mapper (ORM)** and **ActiveRecord** implementation, called **Eloquent**, which is similar to what you will find in Ruby on Rails, to help you define interconnected models. Both the query builder and the ORM are compatible with different databases, such as PostgreSQL, SQLite, MySQL, and SQL Server.

- **Schema builder, migrations, and seeding**: Also inspired by Rails, these features allow you to define your database schema in PHP code and keep track of any changes with the help of database migrations. A migration is a simple way of describing a schema change and how to revert to it. Seeding allows you to populate the selected tables of your database, for example, after running a migration.

- **Template engine**: Partly inspired by the **Razor** template language in ASP. NET MVC, Laravel ships with **Blade**, a lightweight template language with which you can create hierarchical layouts with predefined blocks in which dynamic content is injected.

- **E-mailing**: With its `Mail` class, which wraps the popular `SwiftMailer` library, Laravel makes it very easy to send an e-mail, even with rich content and attachments from your application. Laravel also comes with drivers for popular e-mail sending services such as SendGrid, Mailgun, and Mandrill.

- **Authentication**: Since user authentication is such a common feature in web applications, out of the box Laravel comes with a default implementation to register, authenticate, and even send password reminders to users.

- **Redis**: This is an in-memory key-value store that has a reputation for being extremely fast. If you give Laravel a `Redis` instance that it can connect to, it can use it as a session and general purpose cache, and also give you the possibility to interact with it directly.

- **Queues**: Laravel integrates with several queue services, such as Amazon SQS, Beanstalkd, and IronMQ, to allow you to delay resource-intensive tasks, such as the e-mailing of a large number of users, and run them in the background, rather than keep the user waiting for the task to complete.

- **Event and command bus**: Although not new in version 5, Laravel has brought a command bus to the forefront in which it's easy to dispatch events (a class that represents something that's happened in your application), handle commands (another class that represents something that should happen in your application), and act upon these at different points in your application's lifecycle.

Expressiveness and simplicity

Something that is at the core of Laravel is its philosophy that code should be named simply and expressively. Consider the following code example:

```php
<?php

Route::get('area/{area}', function($area) {
  if (51 == $area && ! Auth::check()) {
    return Redirect::guest('login');
  } else {
    return 'Welcome to Area '.$area;
  }
})->where('area, '[0-9]+');
```

> **Downloading the example code**
>
> You can download the example code files for all Packt Publishing books you have purchased from your account at http://www.packtpub.com. If you purchased this book elsewhere, you can visit http://www.packtpub.com/support and register to have the files e-mailed directly to you.

Even though we have not even touched Laravel or covered its routing functions yet, you will probably have a rough idea of what this snippet of code does. Expressive code is more readable for someone new to a project, and it is probably also easier for you to learn and remember.

Prettifying PHP

Prettifying PHP as well as ensuring code in Laravel is named to effectively convey its actions in plain English, the authors of Laravel have also gone on to apply these principles to existing PHP language functions. A prime example is the `Storage` class, which was created to make file manipulations:

- **More expressive**: To find out when a file was last modified, use `Storage::lastModified($path)` instead of `filemtime(realpath($path))`. To delete a file, use `Storage::delete($path)` instead of `unlink($path)`, which is the plain old PHP equivalent.

- **More consistent**: Some of the original file manipulation functions of PHP are prefixed with `file_`, while others just start with `file`; some are abbreviated and other are not. Using Laravel's wrappers, you no longer need to guess or refer to PHP's documentation.

- **More testable**: Many of the original functions can be tricky to use in tests, due to the exceptions they throw and also because they are more difficult to mock.

- **More feature complete**: This is achieved by adding functions that did not exist before, such as `File::copyDirectory($directory, $destination)`.

There are very rare instances where expressiveness is foregone in the favor of brevity. This is the case for commonly-used shortcut functions, such as `e()`, that escape HTML entities, or `dd()`, with which you can halt the execution of the script and dump the contents of one or more variables.

Responsibilities, naming, and conventions

At the beginning of this chapter, we pointed out that one of the main issues with standard PHP applications was the lack of a clear separation of concerns; business logic becomes entangled with the presentation and data tier. Like many other frameworks that favor convention over configuration, Laravel gives you scaffolding with predefined places to put code in. To help you eliminate trivial decisions, it expects you to name your variables, methods, or database tables in certain ways, even though these are editable via configuration. It is, however, far less opinionated than a framework such as Ruby on Rails and in areas like routing, where there is often more than one way to solve a problem.

You might remember us mentioning that Laravel is a framework that is based on the MVC paradigm. Do not worry if you have not used this architectural pattern before; in a nutshell, this is what you need to know about MVC in order to be able to build your first Laravel applications:

- **Models**: Models represent *resources* in your application. More often than not, they correspond to records in a data store, most commonly a database table. In this respect, you can think of models as representing *entities* in your application, be that a user, a news article, or an event, among others. In Laravel, models are classes that usually extend Eloquent's base `Model` class and are named in **CamelCase** (that is, `NewsArticle`). This will correspond to a database table with the same name, but in **snake_case** and plural (that is, `news_articles`). By default, Eloquent also expects a primary key named `id`, and will also look for—and automatically update—the `created_at` and `updated_at` columns. Models can also describe the relationships they have with other models. For example, a `NewsArticle` model might be associated with a `User` model, as a `User` model might be able to author a `NewsArticle` model. However, models can also refer to data from other data sources, such as an `XML` file, or the response from a web service or API.

- **Controllers or routes**: Controllers, at their simplest, take a request, do something, and then send an appropriate response. Controllers are where the actual processing of data goes, whether that is retrieving data from a database, or handling a form submission, and saving data back to a database. Although you are not forced to adhere to any rules when it comes to creating controller classes in Laravel, it does offer you two sane approaches: RESTful controllers and resource controllers. A RESTful controller allows you to define your own actions and what HTTP methods they should respond to. Resource controllers are based around an entity and allow you to perform common operations on that entity, based on the HTTP method used. Another option is to bypass using controller classes altogether and instead write your logic in your routes, by way of anonymous functions.

- **Views or Templates**: Views are responsible for displaying the response returned from a controller in a suitable format, usually as an HTML web page. They can be conveniently built by using the Blade template language or by simply using standard PHP. The file extension of the view, either `.blade.php` or simply `.php`, determines whether or not Laravel treats your view as a `Blade` template or not.

The following diagram illustrates the interactions between all the constituents applied in a typical web application:

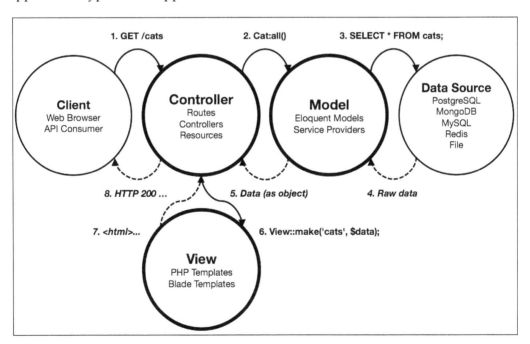

Of course, it is possible to go against the MVC paradigm and the framework's conventions and write code as you wish, but this will often require more effort on the developer's part for no gain.

Helping you become a better developer

Laravel has become a standard-bearer for a new way of developing PHP applications through various design decisions and philosophies, such as the way in which it advocates developers to write framework-agnostic code and to rely on contracts (interfaces) rather than implementations are only a good thing. It has also built such a strong community that it is undoubtedly one of its strongest assets and a major contributing factor to its success; it is possible to get answers within minutes from other users via avenues such as forums, IRC, and social networking websites like Twitter.

However, if time has taught us anything, it is that frameworks come and go and it is hard to predict when Laravel will lose its steam and be supplanted by a better or more popular framework. Nonetheless, Laravel will not only make you more productive in the short term, but it also has the potential to make you a better developer in the long run. By using it to build web applications, you will indirectly become more familiar with the following concepts, all of which are highly transferable to any other programming language or framework. These include the MVC paradigm and **Object-oriented programming** (**OOP**) design patterns, the use of dependency managers, testing and dependency injection, and the power and limitations of ORMs and database migration.

It will also inspire you to write more expressive code with descriptive **DocBlock** comments that facilitate the generation of documentation, as well as the future maintenance of the application, irrespective of whether it is done by you or another developer.

Structure of a Laravel application

Over the course of the next two chapters, we will install Laravel and create our first application. Like most frameworks, Laravel starts out with a complete directory tree for you to organize your code in, and also includes placeholder files for you to use as a starting point. Here is what the directory of a new Laravel 5 application looks like:

```
./app/                      # Your Laravel application
  ./app/Commands/           # Commands classes   ./app/Console/
    ./app/Console/Commands/ # Command-line scripts
  ./app/Events/             # Events that your application can
    raise
  ./app/Exceptions/
```

```
    ./app/Handlers/              # Exception handlers
      ./app/Handlers/Commands    # Handlers for command classes
      ./app/Handlers/Events      # Handlers for event classes
    ./app/Http/
      ./app/Http/Controllers/    # Your application's controllers
      ./app/Http/Middleware/     # Filters applied to requests
      ./app/Http/Requests/       # Classes that can modify requests
      ./app/Http/routes.php      # URLs and their corresponding
                                   handlers
    ./app/Providers              # Service provider classes
    ./app/Services               # Services used in your application

  ./bootstrap/                   # Application bootstrapping scripts

  ./config/                      # Configuration files

    ./database/
    ./database/migrations/       # Database migration classes
    ./database/seeds/            # Database seeder classes

  ./public/                    # Your application's document root
  ./public/.htaccess           # Sends incoming requests to index.php
  ./public/index.php           # Starts Laravel application

  ./resources/
    ./resources/assets/          # Hold raw assets like LESS & Sass
                                   files
    ./resources/lang/            # Localization and language files
    ./resources/views/           # Templates that are rendered as HTML

  ./storage/
    ./storage/app/               # App storage, like file uploads etc
    ./storage/framework/         # Framework storage (cache)
    ./storage/logs/              # Contains application-generated logs

  ./tests/                       # Test cases

  ./vendor/                      # Third-party code installed by
                                   Composer
  ./.env.example                 # Example environment variable file

  ./artisan                      # Artisan command-line utility

  ./composer.json                # Project dependencies manifest

  ./phpunit.xml                  # Configures PHPUnit for running
                                   tests

  ./server.php                   # A lightweight local development
                                   server
```

Like Laravel's source code, the naming of directories is also expressive, and it is easy to guess what each directory is for. The app directory is where most of your application's server-side code will reside, which has subdirectories both for how your application could be accessed (Console and Http), as well as subdirectories for organizing code that could be used in both scenarios (such as Events and Services). We will explore the responsibilities of each directory further in the next chapters.

The service container and request lifecycle

Whether you are a beginner in PHP or an experienced developer in a different language, it might not always be obvious how an HTTP request reaches a Laravel application. Indeed, the request lifecycle is fundamentally different from plain PHP scripts that are accessed directly by their URI (for example, GET http://example.com/about-us.php).

The public/ directory is meant to act as the document root; in other words, the directory in which your web server starts looking after every incoming request. Once URL rewriting is properly set up, every request that does not match an existing file or directory hits the /public/index.php file. This file includes the Composer autoloader file, which loads in dependencies (including the Laravel framework components) and also where to look for your application's code. Your application is then bootstrapped, loading configuration variables based on the environment. Once this is done, it instantiates a new service container instance, which in turn handles the incoming request, uses the HTTP method and URL used to access the application (such as POST /comments), and passes the request off to the correct controller action or route for handling.

Exploring Laravel

In this chapter, we are only covering the general mechanisms of how Laravel works, without looking at the detailed implementation examples. For the majority of developers, who just want to get the job done, this is sufficient. Moreover, it is much easier to delve into the source code of Laravel once you have already built a few applications. Nevertheless, here are some answers to the questions that might crop up when exceptions are thrown or when you navigate through the source code. In doing so, you will come across some methods that are not documented in the official guide, and you might even be inspired to write better code.

Browsing the API (`http://laravel.com/api`) can be somewhat intimidating at first. But it is often the best way to understand how a particular method works under the hood. Here are a few tips:

- The `Illuminate` namespace does not refer to a third-party library. It is the namespace that the author of Laravel has chosen for the different modules that constitute Laravel. Every single one of them is meant to be reusable and used independently of the framework.

- When searching for a class definition, for example, `Auth`, in the source code or the API, you might bump into `Facade`, which hardly contains any helpful methods and only acts as a proxy to the real class. This is because almost every dependency in Laravel is injected into the service container when it is instantiated.

- Most of the libraries that are included in the `vendor/` directory contain a `README` file, which details the functionality present in the library (for example, `vendor/nesbot/carbon/readme.md`).

Changes in Version 5 from Version 4

Laravel 5 started life as Laravel 4.3, but was promoted to its own major version when it became apparent that this new version was going to be a radical departure from version 4 of the framework. Laravel 5 builds on Laravel 4 as a base, but makes architecting larger applications with things like an application namespace out of the box. Laravel 4 applications will need a fair bit of work to be ported to Laravel 5. Features that are new or have been updated in Laravel 5 include:

- **Method injection**: In Laravel 4, you could type hint (specify in the constructor) the dependencies a class needed, and Laravel would automatically resolve those dependencies out of its container. Now, Laravel 5 takes that one step further and will also resolve dependencies specified in class methods, as well as class constructors.

- **Form requests**: Laravel 5 introduces form request classes. These classes can be injected into your controller actions. They take the current request, and on it, you can perform data validation and sanitizing and even user authorization (that is, check if the currently-logged in user can perform the requested action). This streamlines validation, meaning you have to do very little, if any, data validation in your controller actions.

- **Socialite**: New to Laravel 5 is an optional package called Socialite that you can declare as a Composer dependency. It makes authenticating with third-party services a breeze, meaning you can easily implement functionality like login with Facebook in a few lines of code.

- **Elixir**: Laravel 5 also looks at making front-end development easier. A lot of developers these days are using languages like LESS and Sass to create their style sheets, and concatenating JavaScript files into one, minified JavaScript file to reduce HTTP requests and speed up loading times. Elixir is a wrapper around **Gulp**, a **Node.js** based build system that simplifies the tasks mentioned here. This greatly reduces the time needed to get up and running with a new application, as you don't have to install Node.js modules or Gulp files from other projects. You get it free from the get-go.

Summary

In this chapter, we have introduced you to Laravel 5 and how it can help you to write better, more structured applications while reducing the amount of boilerplate code. We have also explained the concepts and PHP features used by Laravel, and you should now be well equipped to get started and write your first application!

In the next chapter, you will learn how to set up an environment in which you can develop Laravel applications and you will also be introduced to Composer for managing dependencies.

2
Setting Up a Development Environment

Laravel is more than just a framework: a whole ecosystem and toolset has been developed around it to make building PHP applications faster and more enjoyable. These tools are entirely opt-in and the knowledge of them is not necessary to use and build projects in Laravel, but they do go hand-in-hand with the framework, so it's worth covering.

In this chapter, we will cover the following topics:

- Meeting Composer, a dependency manager
- Introduction to Homestead, and using it to manage Laravel projects

Meeting Composer

In the previous chapter, you discovered that Laravel is built on top of several third-party packages. Rather than including these external dependencies in its own source code, Laravel uses a dependency manager called **Composer** to download them and keep them up to date. Since Laravel is made up of multiple packages, they too are downloaded and installed each time you create a new Laravel project.

Strongly inspired by popular dependency managers in other languages, such as Ruby's Bundler or Node.js's **Node Package Manager** (**npm**), Composer brings these features to PHP and has quickly become the de facto dependency manager in PHP.

A few years ago, you may have used **PHP Extension and Application Repository (PEAR)** to download libraries. PEAR differs from Composer, in that PEAR would install packages on a system-level basis, whereas a dependency manager, such as Composer, installs them on a project-level basis. With PEAR, you could only have one version of a package installed on a system. Composer allows you to use different versions of the same package in different applications, even if they reside on the same system.

Working with the command line

If you are just getting started with web development, you might not be completely familiar with the **command-line interface** (**CLI**). Working with Composer, virtual machines, and Homestead, and later on with **Artisan**, Laravel's CLI utility, will require some interaction with it.

Here is how you can start with CLI:

1. On Windows, look for the **Command Prompt** program. If you cannot find it, just navigate to **Start | Run** and type in `cmd.exe`.

2. On Mac OS X, CLI is called **Terminal**, and it can be found at `/Applications/Utilities`.

3. On Linux, depending on your distribution of Linux, it will be called **Terminal** or **Konsole**, but if you are running Linux, you are probably already familiar with it.

You do not need to have any advanced command-line skills to get through this book and build applications with Laravel. You will, however, need to be able to navigate to the right directory in your file system before running commands. To do this, just enter the `cd` command, followed by the path to your code directory.

 On most systems, you can also just enter `cd`, followed by a space, and then drag and drop the directory into the terminal, as shown here:

```
$ cd /path/to/your/code/directory
```

Otherwise, you can run the following command line on Windows:

```
> cd C:\path\to\your\code\directory
```

If the path contains spaces, then be sure to include it in double quotes to ensure spaces are escaped:

```
> cd "C:\path\to\your\Laravel Projects"
```

In the rest of this book, unless the example is specific to Windows, we will always use the $ character to denote a shell command and use slashes as directory separators. Make sure you adapt the command accordingly, if you are running Windows.

Meet Homestead

If you wanted to develop PHP applications on your personal computer, you needed to have a web server installed and running locally. PHP is installed to interpret your scripts, and other utilities your website may need, such as working with a database. Your website or web application may even have a requirement for other services such as **Memcached** or **Redis**, which are popular caching systems. This saw the rise of utilities such as **WampServer** and **MAMP** to create environments for developing dynamic websites without getting connected to the Internet, but these required configuring.

Building on from installed environments like these, the recommended practice for developing dynamic websites and applications is to use **virtual machines** (**VMs**). These allow you to emulate your production web server's setup on your local machine. You can also use differently configured VMs for different projects—with a WAMP- or MAMP-like setup, every project had to use the same version of PHP, MySQL, and anything else you installed.

The creators of Laravel have created an official Vagrant box called **Homestead**. **Vagrant** is software that allows you to create virtual development environments on your personal computer. You can install Homestead and start creating Laravel projects right away. And if you don't need it any more, you can just remove it from your machine, without anything else being affected. Best of all, if you are currently using a globally installed development environment such as WAMP or MAMP, Homestead won't conflict with it.

Installing Homestead

Homestead is a Vagrant-based VM. Therefore, before using it you will need to install two utilities:

- **VirtualBox** (https://www.virtualbox.org/wiki/Downloads)
- **Vagrant** (http://www.vagrantup.com/downloads.html)

Both have installers for Windows, Mac OS X, and Linux that will guide you through the installation process. To install Homestead, follow these steps:

1. One of the best things about Homestead is that it is hosted on Packagist. This means you can install it via Composer by using the following command:

```
> $ composer global require "laravel/homestead=~2.0"
```

2. Once downloaded, you need to initialize the VM using the following command (you may need to add Homestead to your path first, if you are using Windows):

```
> $ homestead init
```

3. This will create a configuration file that you can edit to point to your projects, as well as create any databases you may need. To edit this file, you can run the following command:

```
> $ homestead edit
```

4. The file will open in your default text editor. When it does, you will see the file is organized into sections. To get up and running, the two sections of most importance are the `folders` section and the `sites` section:

   ○ `folders`: This specifies the directory that you want to be shared on the VM.

   ○ `sites`: This allows you to map a domain to a folder on the Homestead VM, similar to Apache Virtual Hosts.

5. Once you have configured your shared folders and sites, you can boot the VM with the following command:

> `$ homestead up`

6. Finally, you need to add the VM's IP address to your computer's hosts file. The location of this file differs, depending on the platform you're using.

   ○ On Windows, it is located at `C:\Windows\System32\Drivers\etc\hosts`.

   ○ On a *nix system (such as Mac OS X and Linux), it can be found at `/etc/hosts`.

7. Usually, you would need to be an administrator to edit this file. On Mac OS X and Linux, you can open the file with elevated permissions by using the following command:

> `$ sudo open /etc/hosts`

8. You might be prompted for an administrator's password. In your hosts file, add the following line to the bottom:

`192.168.10.10   homesteap.app`

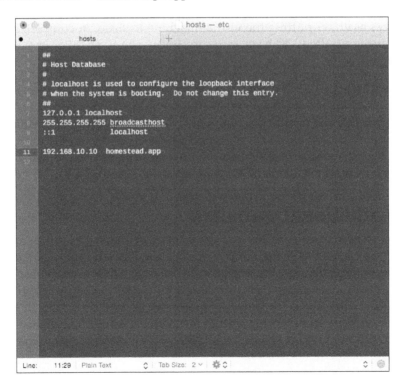

9. Now, if in a web browser you try to visit http://homestead.app, instead of your browser trying to find a website with the domain, it will try to find the website on the machine with the specified IP address. In this instance, the IP address will belong to your Homestead VM and serve the site you've configured for that domain in your configuration file.

 For more information on Homestead and advanced configuration, you can view the official documentation at http://laravel.com/docs/master/homestead.

Everyday usage of Homestead

There are various commands that you can use to interact with your Homestead virtual machine. For example, if the virtual machine is running, how do you stop it? There are two ways.

The first method is with the $ homestead suspend command. This will save the current state of your VM, and allow you to $ homestead resume at a later point in time. Alternatively, you can issue the $ homestead halt command, which will shut down the virtual machine and discard anything in memory. You can think of the differences as either putting the virtual machine to sleep, or completely shutting it down. To bring a halted VM back, you can simply run the $ homestead up command again.

You can also interact and run commands on the virtual machine via the command line. You can SSH into Homestead just like you would an external server. Instead of having to remember the virtual machine's host name and your credentials though, there's a handy $ homestead ssh command that will connect to the machine and then place you in a command prompt ready and waiting. If you are using Windows, there are various tools to execute SSH commands, such as **PuTTY**.

Adding additional websites

One of Homestead's benefits is that you can host more than one application on it. This means you can run as many Laravel applications on it as you want (subject to constraints such as disk space). The process for each site is to map the directory between your host machine and the virtual machine, and to configure nginx to look in this directory when a specific domain name is requested. To do this by hand would mean editing various configuration files, which would become tedious if we needed to do this on a regular basis. Thankfully, Homestead comes with a handy script to make adding new sites a breeze.

You first need to start a new SSH session as mentioned before. Then, run the following script:

```
serve example.app /home/vagrant/Code/example.app/public
```

Replace `example.app` with the host name you want to use. Then, add a new line to your hosts file and you are good to go!

Connecting to your databases

Homestead runs a MySQL instance, which contains the data for all of your configured applications. Laravel exposes the port of the MySQL server via port forwarding, which means you can connect to it from your host machine by using a database management tool such as **Navicat**, **Sequel Pro**, or **MySQL Workbench**. To connect, all you have to do is specify the following parameters:

- **Host**: 127.0.0.1
- **Port**: 33060
- **Username**: homestead
- **Password**: secret

Once connected, you can then browse all of the databases on the Homestead virtual machine, tables, and data, just as you would if the MySQL server was installed on your machine.

Homestead also ships with a **PostgreSQL** database server. Connecting is the same as with the MySQL database server, but you instead use port `54320`.

Creating a new Laravel application

With Homestead set up, you now have a development environment to build Laravel applications that can easily be removed at a later date without disturbing your machine. You must be itching to get started with Laravel, so here we go!

In the next chapter, we will go through building a simple application in Laravel from start to finish. So now, we will prepare this project in Homestead:

1. First, check whether Homestead is running by using the following command:

   ```
   > $ homestead status
   ```

2. If the status is anything other than running, bring it up with the `homestead reload` command. We now need to add our site. It will be a browsable database of cat profiles, so let's call it "Furbook" and give it the fictional domain name of `furbook.com`.

3. We can set this up in Homestead by editing the configuration file and adding the following mappings:

```
sites:
    - map: dev.furbook.com
      to: /home/vagrant/Code/furbook.com/public
databases:
    - furbook
```

4. Run $ `homestead reload`, which should reprovision the sites and also create a new, empty database.

5. Now with our workspace prepared, we need to actually create a new Laravel project. To do this, we need to SSH into our running VM. Homestead makes this incredibly simple:

```
> $ homestead ssh
```

6. This will create a new SSH session and log us in to the running Homestead VM instance. We can now run a Composer command to create a brand new Laravel project as follows:

```
$ cd /home/vagrant/Code/furbook.com
$ composer create-project laravel/laravel . --prefer-dist
```

This will create a new Laravel skeleton project, as well as download all of the libraries that make up the Laravel framework.

Summary

In this chapter, we have begun working with the command line. We've installed Composer and looked at how a dependency manager such as Composer aids development by utilizing prebuilt packages in our projects (of which the Laravel framework is one). We've looked at the concept of virtual machines for developing in, and taken a look and installed the official Laravel VM: Homestead.

The next chapter is where the fun begins! Now that we have a complete development environment set up and a fresh Laravel application created, we will go through the different steps involved in creating a complete Laravel application.

3
Your First Application

Having learned about Laravel's conventions, working with dependencies using Composer, and setting up a development environment with Homestead, you are now ready to build your first application!

In this chapter, you will use the concepts presented in the previous two chapters in a practical way and learn how to do the following:

- Plan the URLs and entities of your application
- Troubleshoot common issues when getting started
- Define routes and their actions, as well as models and their relationships
- Prepare your database and learn how to interact with it using Eloquent
- Use the Blade template language to create hierarchical layouts

The first step in creating a web application is to identify and define its requirements. Then, once the main features have been decided, we derive the main entities as well as the URL structure of the application. Having a well-defined set of requirements and URLs is also essential for other tasks such as testing; this will be covered later in the book.

A lot of new concepts are presented in this chapter. If you have trouble understanding something or if you are not quite sure where to place a particular snippet of code, you can download the annotated source code of the application from `http://packtpub.com/support`, which will help you to follow along.

Planning our application

We are going to build a browsable database of cat profiles. Visitors will be able to create pages for their cats and fill in basic information such as the name, date of birth, and breed of each cat. This application will implement the default **Create-Retrieve-Update-Delete (CRUD)** operations. We will also create an overview page with the option to filter cats by breed. All of the security, authentication, and permission features are intentionally left out, since they will be covered in the further chapters.

Entities, relationships, and attributes

Firstly, we need to define the *entities* of our application. In broad terms, an entity is a thing (person, place, or object) about which the application should store data. From the requirements, we can extract the following entities and attributes:

- **Cats**: They have a numeric identifier, a name, a date of birth, and a breed
- **Breeds**: They only have an identifier and a name

This information will help us when defining the database schema that will store the entities, relationships, attributes, as well as the models, which are the PHP classes that represent the objects in our database.

The map of our application

We now need to think about the URL structure of our application. Having clean and expressive URLs has many benefits. On a usability level, the application will be easier to navigate and will look less intimidating to the user (descriptive URLs look far more appealing than a lengthy query string). For frequent users, individual pages will be easier to remember or bookmark and, if they contain relevant keywords, they will often rank higher in search engine results.

To fulfill the initial set of requirements, we are going to need the following routes in our application. A route is a URL and HTTP method to which the application will respond.

Method	Route	Description
GET	/	Index
GET	/cats	Overview page
GET	/cats/breeds/:name	Overview page for specific breed
GET	/cats/:id	Individual cat page
GET	/cats/create	Form to create a new cat page
POST	/cats	Handle creation of new cat page

Method	Route	Description
GET	/cats/:id/edit	Form to edit existing cat page
PUT	/cats/:id	Handle updates to cat page
GET	/cats/:id/delete	Form to confirm deletion of page
DELETE	/cats/:id	Handle deletion of cat page

You will shortly learn how Laravel helps us to turn this routing sketch into actual code. If you have written PHP applications without a framework, you can briefly reflect on how you would have implemented such a routing structure. To add some perspective, this is what the second to last URL could have looked like with a traditional PHP script (without URL rewriting): `/index.php?p=cats&id=1&_action=delete&confirm=true`.

The preceding table can be prepared using a pen and paper, in a spreadsheet editor, or even in your favorite code editor, using ASCII characters. In the initial development phases, this table of routes is an important prototyping tool that makes you to think about URLs first and helps you define and refine the structure of your application iteratively.

If you have worked with REST APIs, this kind of routing structure will look familiar to you. In RESTful terms, we have a `cats` resource that responds to the different HTTP verbs and provides an additional set of routes to display the necessary forms.

If, on the other hand, you have not worked with RESTful sites, the use of the PUT and DELETE HTTP methods might be new to you. Even though web browsers do not support these methods for standard HTTP requests, Laravel uses a technique that other frameworks such as Rails use, and emulates those methods by adding a `_method` input field to the forms. This way, they can be sent over a standard POST request and are then delegated to the correct route or controller method in the application.

Note also that none of the form submissions endpoints are handled with a GET method. This is primarily because they have side effects; a user can trigger the same action multiple times accidentally when using the browser history. Therefore, when they are called, these routes never display anything to the users. Instead, they redirect them after completing the action (for instance, DELETE `/cats/:id` will redirect the user to GET `/cats`).

Starting the application

Now that we have the blueprints for the application, let's roll up our sleeves and start writing some code.

Start by opening a new terminal window and launch Homestead:

```
$ homestead ssh
```

Navigate to the directory you have mapped to Homestead (by default this is ~/Code):

```
$ cd ~/Code
```

Then use Composer to create a new Laravel project, as follows:

```
$ composer create-project laravel/laravel furbook.com --prefer-dist
$ cd furbook.com
```

Once Composer finishes downloading Laravel and resolving its dependencies, you will have a directory structure identical to the one presented in the first chapter.

Setting the application namespace

Applications in Laravel are namespaced. By default, this is just App—Laravel's great, but it still can't guess the name of your application! To set it to something more appropriate, we can use the Artisan command:

```
$ php artisan app:name Furbook
```

This will update our application's namespace to be Furbook instead.

Writing the first routes

Let's start by writing the first two routes of our application at app/Http/routes. php. This file already contains some comments as well as a couple of sample routes. Remove the existing routes (but leave the opening <?php declaration) before adding the following routes:

```
Route::get('/', function() {
  return 'All cats';
});

Route::get('cats/{id}', function($id) {
  return sprintf('Cat #%s', $id);
});
```

The first parameter of the get method is the URI pattern. When a pattern is matched, the closure function in the second parameter is executed with any parameters that were extracted from the pattern. Note that the slash prefix in the pattern is optional; however, you should not have any trailing slashes. You can make sure that your routes work by opening your web browser and visiting http://dev.furbook.com/cats/123.

Restricting the route parameters

In the pattern of the second route, {id} currently matches any string or number. To restrict it so that it only matches numbers, we can chain a where method to our route as follows:

```
Route::get('cats/{id}', function($id) {
  sprintf('Cat #%d', $id);
})->where('id', '[0-9]+');
```

The where method takes two arguments: the first one is the name of the parameter and the second one is the regular expression pattern that it needs to match.

If you now try to visit an invalid URL, nginx (the server software serving the application) will display a **404 Not Found** error page.

Handling HTTP exceptions

When an error occurs in your application, Laravel raises an exception. This is also true for HTTP errors, as Laravel will raise an appropriate HTTP exception. Usually when an HTTP error occurs, you will want to display a response informing the user what went wrong. This is easy in Laravel 5, as all you need to do is create a view named after the HTTP status code you want it to display for in the resources/views/errors directory.

For example, if you wanted to display a view for **404 Not Found** errors, then all you need to do is create a view at resources/views/errors/404.blade.php.

You can use this approach to handle other HTTP errors as well, such as **403 Forbidden** errors; simply create a view at resources/views/errors/403.blade.php.

We'll cover views later on in this chapter. In the meantime, you can find a list of HTTP status codes at http://en.wikipedia.org/wiki/List_of_HTTP_status_codes.

Performing redirections

It is also possible to redirect visitors using the redirect() helper in your routes. If, for example, we wanted everyone to be redirected to /cats when they visit the application for the first time, we would write the following lines of code:

```
Route::get('/', function() {
  return redirect('cats');
});
```

Now, we can create the route for the URL we're redirecting to:

```
Route::get('cats', function() {
    return 'All cats';
});
```

Returning views

The most frequent object that you will return from your routes is the `View` object. Views receive data from a route (or controller action) and inject it into a template, therefore helping you to separate the business and presentation logic in your application.

To add your first view, simply create a file called `about.php` at `resources/views` and add the following content to it:

```
<h2>About this site</h2>
There are over <?php echo $number_of_cats; ?> cats on this site!
```

Then, return the view using the `view()` helper function with the variable, `$number_of_cats`:

```
Route::get('about', function() {
    return view('about')->with('number_of_cats', 9000);
});
```

Finally, visit `/about` in your browser to see the rendered view. This view was written with plain PHP; however, Laravel comes with a powerful template language called Blade, which will be introduced later in this chapter.

Preparing the database

Before we can expand the functionality of our routes, we need to define the models of our application, prepare the necessary database schema, and populate the database with some initial data.

Homestead ships with a MySQL server built in, so we can use MySQL for our database; however, it does require a little bit of configuration first, before we can use a MySQL database in our application.

The first step is to open our application's configuration file, which should have been created at `.env` when we created the application with Composer. Find the line that says `DB_DATABASE=homestead` and change it to `DB_DATABASE=furbook`.

We can also add the database name to our Homestead configuration file, so that the database is created automatically for us. Open the file from the command line, using the following command:

```
$ homestead edit
```

Under the databases section, add a new line:

```
databases:
    - homestead
    - furbook
```

Save the file, then run the homestead provision command to create the database.

Creating Eloquent models

The first and easiest step is to define the models with which our application is going to interact. At the beginning of this chapter, we identified two main entities: *cats* and *breeds*. Laravel ships with Eloquent, a powerful ORM that lets you define these entities, map them to their corresponding database tables, and interact with them using PHP methods, rather than raw SQL. By convention, they are written in the singular form; a model named Cat will map to the cats table in the database, and a hypothetical Mouse model will map to the mice table. You can also manually define the name of the database table using the aptly-named $table property, in case your table name doesn't follow the convention expected by Laravel:

```
protected $table = 'custom_table_name';
```

The Cat model, saved at app/Cat.php, will have a belongsTo relationship with the Breed model, which is defined in the following code snippet:

```php
<?php namespace Furbook;

use Illuminate\Database\Eloquent\Model;

class Cat extends Model {
  protected $fillable = ['name','date_of_birth','breed_id'];
  public function breed() {
    return $this->belongsTo('Furbook\Breed');
  }
}
```

The `$fillable` array defines the list of fields that Laravel can fill by **mass assignment**, which is a convenient way to assign attributes to a model. By convention, the column that Laravel will use to find the related model has to be called `breed_id` in the database. The `Breed` model, `app/Breed.php`, is defined with the inverse `hasMany` relationship as follows:

```php
<?php namespace Furbook;

use Illuminate\Database\Eloquent\Model;

class Breed extends Model {
  public $timestamps = false;
  public function cats(){
    return $this->hasMany('Furbook\Cat');
  }
}
```

By default, Laravel expects a `created_at` and `updated_at` timestamp field in the database table. Since we are not interested in storing these timestamps with the breeds, we disable them in the model by setting the `$timestamps` property to `false`:

```php
protected $timestamps = false;
```

This is the entire code that is required in our models for now. We will discover various other features of Eloquent as we progress in this book; however, in this chapter, we will primarily use two methods: `all()` and `find()`. To illustrate their purpose, here are the SQL queries that they generate:

```
Furbook\Breed::all()      => SELECT * FROM breeds;
Furbook\Cat::find(1)      => SELECT * FROM cats WHERE id = 1;
```

The properties of an Eloquent model can be retrieved with the `->` operator: `$cat->name`. The same goes for the properties of the related models, which are accessible with: `$cat->breed->name`. Behind the scenes, Eloquent will perform the necessary SQL joins.

Building the database schema

Now that we have defined our models, we need to create the corresponding database schema. Thanks to Laravel's support for migrations and its powerful schema builder, you will not have to write any SQL code and you will also be able to keep track of any schema changes in a version control system. To create your first migration, open a new terminal window and enter the following command:

```
$ php artisan make:migration create_breeds_table --create=breeds
```

This will create a new migration at `database/migrations/`. If you open the newly created file, you will find some code that Laravel has generated for you. Migrations always have an `up()` and `down()` method that defines the schema changes when migrating up or down. Migrating up is modifying the database schema (that is, adding a table at a later date), whereas, migrating down is the process of undoing that schema change. By convention, the table and field names are written in snake_case. Also, the table names are written in plural form.

Our `breeds` table migration will look like this:

```
public function up() {
  Schema::create('breeds', function($table) {
    $table->increments('id');
    $table->string('name');
  });
}
public function down() {
  Schema::drop('breeds');
}
```

We can repeat the process to also create our `cats` table schema:

```
public function up() {
  Schema::create('cats', function($table) {
    $table->increments('id');
    $table->string('name');
    $table->date('date_of_birth');
    $table->integer('breed_id')->unsigned()->nullable();
    $table->foreign('breed_id')->references('id')->on('breeds');
  });
}
public function down() {
  Schema::drop('cats');
}
```

The `date()` and `string()` methods create fields with the corresponding types (in this case, DATE and VARCHAR) in the database, `increments()` creates an auto-incrementing INTEGER primary key, and `timestamps()` adds the `created_at` and `updated_at` DATETIME fields that Eloquent expects, by default. The `nullable()` method specifies that the column can have NULL values.

Laravel offers the following methods for defining migrations:

Command	Description
`$table->bigIncrements('name');`	It creates an auto-incrementing big integer column
`$table->bigInteger('name');`	It creates a BIGINT column
`$table->binary('name');`	It creates a BLOB column
`$table->boolean('active');`	It creates a BOOLEAN column
`$table->char('name', 8);`	It creates a CHAR column with the given length
`$table->date('birthdate');`	It creates a DATE column
`$table->dateTime('created_at');`	It creates a DATETIME column
`$table->decimal('amount', 5, 2);`	It creates a DECIMAL column with the given precision and scale
`$table->double('column', 10, 5);`	It creates a DOUBLE column, with 10 digits in total and 5 after the decimal point
`$table->enum('gender', ['Female', 'Male']);`	It creates an ENUM column
`$table->float('amount');`	It creates a FLOAT column
`$table->increments('id');`	It creates an auto-incrementing integer column
`$table->integer('rating');`	It creates an INTEGER column
`$table->json('options');`	It creates a JSON column
`$table->longText('description');`	It creates a LONGTEXT column
`$table->mediumInteger('name');`	It creates a MEDIUMINT column
`$table->mediumText('name');`	It creates a MEDIUMTEXT column
`$table->morphs('taggable');`	It creates two columns: INTEGER taggable_id and STRING taggable_type
`$table->nullableTimestamps();`	This is similar to timestamps (next), but allows NULL values
`$table->rememberToken();`	It adds a remember_token VARCHAR column
`$table->tinyInteger('name');`	It creates a TINYINT column
`$table->softDeletes();`	It adds a deleted_at column for soft deletes
`$table->string('name');`	It creates a VARCHAR column
`$table->string('name', 255);`	It creates a VARCHAR column of the given length
`$table->text('name');`	It creates a TEXT column
`$table->time('name');`	It creates a TIME column
`$table->timestamp('name');`	It creates a TIMESTAMP column
`$table->timestamps();`	It creates created_at and deleted_at columns

We've also created a foreign key in the `cats` migration. This links the `breed_id` column value to an ID in the `breeds` table. This is so that we don't have to keep specifying the breed name over and over again. We can just reference one record in the `breeds` table. If that record is updated, then all `cats` linked to it will also be updated.

To run both of the migrations, enter the following command:

```
$ php artisan migrate
```

When it is run for the first time, this command will also create a `migrations` table that Laravel will use to keep track of the migrations that have been run. It will then run any outstanding migrations. On subsequent runs, the command will use the `migrations` table to determine if any migration files need running, and run them, if so.

We created our `breeds` table migration before the `cats` table migration because we have a **foreign key** in our `cats` table. If we were to try and create the `cats` table first, it will fail as the column it is referencing does not exist yet.

Seeding the database

Rather than manually populating our database, we can use the seeding helpers offered by Laravel. This time, there is no Artisan command to generate the file, but all we need to do is create a new class called `BreedsTableSeeder.php` at `database/seeds/`. This class extends Laravel's `Seeder` class and defines the following `run()` method:

```
class BreedsTableSeeder extends Seeder {
  public function run() {
    DB::table('breeds')->insert([
      ['id' => 1, 'name' => "Domestic"],
      ['id' => 2, 'name' => "Persian"],
      ['id' => 3, 'name' => "Siamese"],
      ['id' => 4, 'name' => "Abyssinian"],
    ]);
  }
}
```

You can bulk insert an array but you can also insert arbitrary code in the `run()` method to load data from say, a CSV or JSON file. There are also third-party libraries that can help you generate large amounts of test data to fill your database, such as the excellent Faker.

To control the order of execution of the seeders, Laravel lets you call them individually at `database/seeds/DatabaseSeeder.php`. In our case, since we only have one seeder, all we need to write is the following line:

```
$this->call('BreedsTableSeeder');
```

Then, we can seed the database by calling it, using the following command:

```
$ php artisan db:seed
```

Seeding is good for initially populating a database. If we were to re-run the seed command, we would actually get an error as we're defining primary keys for our records; if we tried re-seeding, the database will trigger a duplicate primary key error. We can first truncate the table, but this will be dangerous if deployed to a production environment, as it will delete any user-contributed records, as well as your seed data definitions!

Mastering Blade

Now that we have some information in our database, we need to define the templates that are going to display it. Blade is Laravel's lightweight template language and its syntax is very easy to learn. Here are some examples of how Blade can reduce the number of keystrokes and increase the readability of your templates:

Standard PHP syntax	Blade syntax
`<?php echo $var; ?>`	`{!! $var !!}`
`<?php echo htmlentities($var); ?>`	`{{ $var }}`
`<?php if ($cond): ?>…<?php endif; ?>`	`@if ($cond) … @endif`

If you use the default double braces notation, then variables are escaped. This is to protect against XSS vulnerabilities (explained in more detail in *Chapter 7, Authentication and Security*). If you really need the raw value of variable un-escaped, then you can use single braces, with two exclamation marks inside on each side. You should only do this if you trust the value that the variable contains.

Blade also supports all of PHP's major constructs to create loops and conditions: `@for`, `@foreach`, `@while`, `@if`, and `@elseif`, allowing you to avoid opening and closing the `<?php` tags everywhere in your templates.

Creating a master view

Blade lets you build hierarchical layouts by allowing the templates to be nested and extended. The following code snippet is the **master** template that we are going to use for our application. We will save it as `resources/views/layouts/master.blade.php`.

```
<!DOCTYPE html>
<html lang="en">
  <head>
```

```
      <meta charset="utf-8" />
      <title>Furbook</title>
      <link rel="stylesheet" href="{{ asset('css/bootstrap.min.css')
        }}">
  </head>
  <body>
    <div class="container">
      <div class="page-header">
        @yield('header')
      </div>
      @if (Session::has('success'))
        <div class="alert alert-success">
          {{ Session::get('success') }}
        </div>
      @endif
      @yield('content')
    </div>
  </body>
</html>
```

The Bootstrap CSS framework is included to speed up the prototyping of the application interface. You can download it from `http://getbootstrap.com` and place the minified CSS file at `public/css/`. To ensure that its path prefix is set correctly, even when Laravel is run from a subfolder, we use the `asset()` helper. You can see the complete list of Blade template helpers that are available to you, visit `http://laravel.com/docs/helpers`.

To inform the user about the outcome of certain actions, we have prepared a notification area between the header and the page content. This **flash data** (in other words, the session data that is only available for the next request) is passed and retrieved to and from the `Session` object.

The `@yield` directives act as placeholders for the different sections that a child view can populate and override. To see how a child template can re-use them, we are going to recreate the `about` view by changing its extension to `.blade.php` and extending our `master` layout template instead:

```
@extends('layouts.master')
@section('header')
  <h2>About this site</h2>
@stop
@section('content')
  <p>There are over {{ $number_of_cats }} cats on this site!</p>
@stop
```

The @section ... @stop directives delimit the blocks of content that are going to be injected into the master template. You can see how this is done in the following diagram:

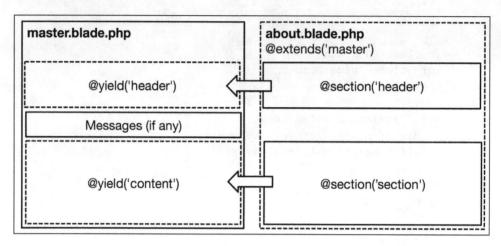

If you now reopen the /about route in your web browser, without changing anything in your previous route definition, you will see the new view. Laravel's view finder will simply use the new file, and since its name ends with .blade.php, treat it like a Blade template.

Back to the routes

Now that we have a main layout template that we can extend and re-use, we can start to create the individual routes of our application at app/Http/routes.php, along with the different views that will display the application data.

The overview page

This is the *index* page that is going to display all of the cats using the cats.index view. We will also re-use this view for the second route where cats are filtered by breed, since both the routes are almost identical. Note that Laravel expects you to use the dot notation (cats.index and not cats/index) to refer to a view located inside a subdirectory:

```
Route::get('cats', function() {
  $cats = Furbook\Cat::all();
  return view('cats.index')->with('cats', $cats);
});
```

```
Route::get('cats/breeds/{name}', function($name) {
    $breed = Furbook\Breed::with('cats')
      ->whereName($name)
      ->first();
    return view('cats.index')
      ->with('breed', $breed)
      ->with('cats', $breed->cats);
});
```

The only novelty in these routes is the slightly more advanced Eloquent queries.
While we already know that the all() method in the first route loads all of the entries
from the cats table, the second route uses a more complex query. The with('cats')
method will load any related cat models. The whereName is a dynamic method that
creates a WHERE SQL clause, which will translate to WHERE name = $name. The long-
hand expression of this will be where('name', '=', $name). Finally, we fetch the
first breed record (and related cat models) with the first() method.

The template, saved at cats/index.blade.php, will look like this:

```
@extends('layouts.master')

@section('header')
  @if (isset($breed))
    <a href="{{ url('/') }}">Back to the overview</a>
  @endif
<h2>
  All @if (isset($breed)){{ $breed->name }}@endif Cats

  <a href="{{ url('cats/create') }}" class="btn btn-primary
    pull-right">
    Add a new cat
  </a>
</h2>
@stop
@section('content')
  @foreach ($cats as $cat)
    <div class="cat">
      <a href="{{ url('cats/'.$cat->id) }}">
        <strong>{{ $cat->name }}</strong> - {{ $cat->breed->name
          }}
      </a>
    </div>
  @endforeach
@stop
```

With the help of a `foreach` loop, the view iterates over the list of cats that it received from the route. Since we will be using this view to display both the index page (`/cats`) as well as the breed overview page (`/cats/breeds/{breed}`), we used the `@if` directives in two places to conditionally display more information.

Displaying a cat's page

The next route is used to display a single cat. To find a cat by its ID, we use Eloquent's `find()` method:

```
Route::get('cats/{id}', function($id) {
  $cat = Furbook\Cat::find($id);
  return view('cats.show) ->with('cat', $cat);
});
```

Route-model binding

Route-model binding is the method of automatically transforming a route parameter to a model instance, so we don't have to manually retrieve the model. Since this is such a common pattern, Laravel provides you with a way to automatically bind a model to a route and, therefore, make your code shorter and more expressive. To bind the `$cat` variable to the `Cat` model, open `app/Providers/RouteServiceProvider.php`. Modify the `boot()` method so that it looks like this:

```
public function boot(Router $router) {
  parent::boot($router);
  $router->model('cat', 'Furbook\Cat');
}
```

This allows you to shorten your route and pass a `Cat` object to it instead:

```
Route::get('cats/{cat}', function(Furbook\Cat $cat) {
  return view('cats.show')->with('cat', $cat);
});
```

The view, `cats/show.blade.php`, does not contain any new directives. It simply displays the name of the cat with the links to edit or delete it. In the `content` section, we return its age and breed if the breed is set; this is shown in the following snippet:

```
@extends('layouts.master')

@section('header')
  <a href="{{ url('/') }}">Back to overview</a>
  <h2>
      {{ $cat->name }}
```

```
    </h2>
    <a href="{{ url('cats/'.$cat->id.'/edit') }}">
      <span class="glyphicon glyphicon-edit"></span>
      Edit
    </a>
    <a href="{{ url('cats/'.$cat->id.'/delete') }}">
      <span class="glyphicon glyphicon-trash"></span>
      Delete
    </a>
    <p>Last edited: {{ $cat->updated_at->diffForHumans() }}</p>
  @stop

  @section('content')
    <p>Date of Birth: {{ $cat->date_of_birth }}</p>
    <p>
      @if ($cat->breed)
        Breed:
        {{ link_to('cats/breeds/'.$cat->breed->name,
          $cat->breed->name) }}
      @endif
    </p>
  @stop
```

Adding, editing, and deleting cats

The next series of routes and views will be used to create, edit, and delete a cat page.

Until version 5, Laravel came with a package for creating common HTML and form elements. In Laravel 5 applications, we need to bring this package back into use. We do this via Composer.

In the require section of composer.json, add the following code:

```
"laravelcollective/html": "5.0.*"
```

Then run $ composer update. This will install the package. Next, we need to register the service provider and façades. Open config/app.php and add the following the $providers array:

```
'Collective\Html\HtmlServiceProvider',
```

Then add the following two lines to the $facades array:

```
'Form' => 'Collective\Html\FormFacade',
'HTML' => 'Collective\Html\HtmlFacade',
```

This now gives us a lot of helpful methods with which to build forms in our templates.

Although Blade templates are hierarchical, it is still possible to include other templates in views, as you may be used to doing with the `include()` or `require()` functions in PHP. We will use this to share the form fields needed for both the create and edit templates.

In `resources/views/partials/forms/cat.blade.php`, add the following content:

```
<div class="form-group">
  {!! Form::label('name', 'Name') !!}
  <div class="form-controls">
    {!! Form::text('name', null, ['class' => 'form-control']) !!}
  </div>
</div>
<div class="form-group">
  {!! Form::label('date_of_birth', 'Date of Birth') !!}
  <div class="form-controls">
    {!! Form::date('date_of_birth', null, ['class' =>
      'form-control']) !!}
  </div>
</div>
<div class="form-group">
  {!! Form::label('breed_id', 'Breed') !!}
  <div class="form-controls">
    {!! Form::select('breed_id', $breeds, null, ['class' =>
      'form-control']) !!}
  </div>
</div>
{!! Form::submit('Save Cat', ['class' => 'btn btn-primary']) !!}
```

The `Form::select()` helper builds a `<select>` dropdown with the different choices. It expects the list of choices to be passed to a multidimensional array. Rather than binding this array to each route, we can use **view composers**, another feature of Laravel, which allows you to bind a variable to a specific view each time.

We can initialize a view composer by adding it to our application's service provider. Open `app/Providers/AppServiceProvider.php` and change the `boot()` method to look like this:

```
public function boot(ViewFactory $view) {
  $view->composer('partials.forms.cat',
    'App\Http\Views\Composers\CatFormComposer');
}
```

We also need to resolve `ViewFactory`. At the top of the file, underneath the namespace declaration, add the following line:

```
use Illuminate\Contracts\View\Factory as ViewFactory;
```

We now need to create the actual view composer class. We've specified the path, so let's create the file and add the following code to it:

```php
<?php namespace Furbook\Http\Views\Composers;
use Furbook\Breed;
use Illuminate\Contracts\View\View;

class CatFormComposer {
  protected $breeds;
  public function __construct(Breed $breeds) {
    $this->breeds = $breeds;
  }
  public function compose(View $view) {
    $view->with('breeds', $this->breeds->lists('name', 'id'));
  }
}
```

Now when the `partials.forms.cat` template partial is called, the view composer kicks in. When Laravel instantiates it, it'll read the constructor and automatically inject instances of the specified types. In our view composer's constructor, we specify that we need an instance of our `Breed` model, and then store the instance as a class property.

Once the view composer has been initialized, the `compose()` method is called. This is where the actual binding of data to the view occurs. As our model is an Eloquent model, we can use the `lists()` method that fetches all records in an associative array, which is just what we need for our `select` list. The first parameter is the value that the user will see (the breed name in this instance) and the second parameter is what will be used as the `value` attribute in the `<option>` tag (the breed ID).

Now that we have a partial form with breed options automatically being injected when requested, we can continue on with building the create, edit, and delete views.

The create view is straightforward: we extend out master layout, open our form, and then include the partial we've just created. In `resources/views/cats/create.blade.php`, add the following code:

```
@extends('layouts.master')
@section('header')
  <h2>Add a new cat</h2>
@stop
@section('content')
```

```
   {!! Form::open(['url' => '/cats']) !!}
     @include('partials.forms.cat')
   {!! Form::close() !!}
@stop
```

The edit template (`resources/views/cats/edit.blade.php`) will look similar, barring a few small changes:

```
@extends('layouts.master')
@section('header')
  <h2>Edit a cat</h2>
@stop
@section('content')
   {!! Form::model($cat, ['url' => '/cats/'.$cat->id],
     'method' => 'put') !!}
     @include('partials.forms.cat')
   {!! Form::close() !!}
@stop
```

We didn't include the opening and closing form tags in the partial, as we need to change the action URL and method depending on the action. Also, in the edit template, we're using form-model binding to bind the Cat instance passed to our template, to the form. This automatically populates the values of the form fields with the value of the attributes in our Cat model instance.

Now that we have our views, we can create the corresponding routes:

```
Route::get('cats/create', function() {
  return view('cats.create');
});

Route::post('cats', function() {
  $cat = Furbook\Cat::create(Input::all());
  return redirect('cats/'.$cat->id)
    ->withSuccess('Cat has been created.');
});

Route::get('cats/{cat}/edit', function(Furbook\Cat $cat) {
  return view('cats.edit')->with('cat', $cat);
});

Route::put('cats/{cat}', function(Furbook\Cat $cat) {
  $cat->update(Input::all());
  return redirect('cats/'.$cat->id)
    ->withSuccess('Cat has been updated.');
});
```

```
Route::delete('cats/{cat}', function(Furbook\Cat $cat) {
  $cat->delete();
  return redirect('cats')
    ->withSuccess('Cat has been deleted.');
});
```

You might have noticed that a new method `withSuccess()` is being used in the preceding routes in conjunction with our redirects. This isn't an explicitly defined method; instead, it is an example of **overloading** in Laravel. In the context of redirects, Laravel looks at method calls that have `with` in the beginning; it takes the latter part and assigns it to the session flash data. This includes the session variables that will be available in the next request, and the next request only. This makes it perfect for single-use data such as success messages, as we have seen earlier.

If you look back at our master layout template, you can see the provision we have to check for any session variables with the key `success`; if it exists, we simply display it in a Bootstrap success alert.

Any input data that is received by the application and that you would normally access via the `$_GET` or `$_POST` variables is instead retrievable by using the `Input::get()` method. It is also possible to retrieve an array of all the input data with `Input::all()`. In the `POST /cats` and `PUT /cats/{cat}` routes respectively, we use the `create()` and `update()` methods from Eloquent with `Input::all()` as their argument. This is only possible because we specified the fields that are fillable in the `Cat` model beforehand.

We now have a working application where users can add, edit, and delete cats.

Moving from simple routing to powerful controllers

So far, we have been creating **closure-based routes**. This is great for quickly prototyping applications, and is prevalent in micro-frameworks such as **Silex** and **Slim**; however, as your application grows, this approach might become cumbersome and limiting. The alternative (and recommended) approach to defining the logic to be executed when a route is requested is in controllers, the C in MVC.

A controller is usually a class, containing one or more methods, also known as **actions**. You usually have a route map to a controller action.

Consider the following example:

```
Route::get('user/{id}', ['middleware' => ['auth'], function($id) {
    // Perform some operations
    return 'Something';
}]);
```

To achieve the same functionality with a controller and remove the business logic from the routes, create a new file at `app/Http/Controllers/UserController.php`:

```php
<?php namespace Furbook\Http\Controllers;

class UserController extends Controller {
    public function __construct()
    {
        $this->middleware('auth');
    }
    public function show($id)
    {
        $this->doSomething();
        return 'Something';
    }
    protected function doSomething()
    {
        // Perform some operations
    }
}
```

This approach can greatly improve the reusability and testability of your code, especially if your theoretical `doSomething()` method is used in more than one controller action. You can test it just once in isolation, and then rely on it. When you venture into more advanced topics such as dependency injection, you can even swap entire classes when you instantiate the controller, but we will not cover this here.

Finally, to tell Laravel which controller action to use, simply rewrite the route declaration as follows:

```
Route::get('user/{id}', ['uses' => 'UserController@show']);
```

The root controller namespace (`App\Http\Controllers`) is automatically prepended to the controller class name to avoid the task of specifying it for each and every route.

Resource controllers

Laravel greatly simplifies the creation of REST APIs with resource controllers. Since they adhere to conventions, there is only a limited defined set of actions that can be performed from the controller. In fact, all the routes we created earlier can be rewritten as follows:

```
Route::resource('cat', 'CatController');
```

This will register the following routes:

Verb	Path	Action	Route Name
GET	/cat	index	cat.index
GET	/cat/create	create	cat.create
POST	/cat	store	cat.store
GET	/cat/{id}	show	cat.show
GET	/cat/{id}/edit	edit	cat.edit
PUT/PATCH	/cat/{id}	update	cat.update
DELETE	/cat/{id}	destroy	cat.destroy

Then, in your CatController class, you will have all of the different actions: index, create, show, edit, and so on. These will then be wired up to respond to the correct route and HTTP verb.

You can create a stub resource controller with the following Artisan command:

$ php artisan make:controller CatController

Why not try re-writing the closure-based route actions into your new CatController class?

Summary

We have covered a lot in this chapter. You learned how to define routes, prepare the models of the application, and interact with them. Moreover, we have had a glimpse at the many powerful features of Eloquent, Blade, as well as the other convenient helpers in Laravel to create forms and input fields—all of this in under 200 lines of code!

In the next chapter, you will learn more about Laravel's powerful ORM, Eloquent, which allows you to perform powerful database queries without writing a line of SQL.

4
Eloquent ORM

In the previous chapter, we touched on Eloquent, the **object-relational mapper (ORM)** that ships with Laravel. Eloquent acts as the model layer (the M in MVC) in our applications. As it is such a big part of most applications built in Laravel, we are going to take a look at Eloquent in more detail.

In this chapter, we will cover the following topics:

- Reading and writing data to our database
- Relationships between models
- Query scopes
- Model events and observers
- Collections

Eloquent conventions

Eloquent has some conventions, which, if followed, will make your life easier. This approach is known as **convention over configuration**, which means, if you follow these conventions, you will have to do very little configuration for things to "just work".

An Eloquent model is contained in a single class and is the "studly-cased", singular version of your database table's name. Studly-case is similar to camel-casing, but the first letter is uppercase as well. So if you have a database table called `cats`, then your model class will be called `Cat`.

There is no set place in the filesystem to place your Eloquent models; you are free to organize them as you see fit. You can use an Artisan command to create a model **stub** (a simple class with the basic structure of an Eloquent model). The command is:

```
$ php artisan app:model Cat
```

By default, Artisan places new model classes in the `app` directory. You are free to move your model classes and store them in whatever directory you wish, just be sure to update the namespace declaration at the top of the file to reflect its new location.

Our model stub class will look like this:

```php
<?php namespace App;
use Illuminate\Database\Eloquent\Model;
class Cat extends Model {
    //
}
```

This will attempt to use a table called `cats` by default.

Our model class extends the base Eloquent `Model` class, which contains all of the goodness we're going to use over the course of this chapter. The first thing you should do after creating a model is define the database table it maps to. In our case, the database table will be called `cats`:

```php
class Cat extends Model {
    protected $table = 'cats';
}
```

This is a working Eloquent model at its simplest and you can now use it to fetch records from your database table.

Retrieving data

Eloquent provides you with numerous ways to fetch records from your database, each with their own appropriate use case. You can simply fetch all records in one go; a single record based on its primary key; records based on conditions; or a paginated list of either all or filtered records.

To fetch all records, we can use the aptly-named `all` method:

```php
use App\Cat;
$cats = Cat::all();
```

To fetch a record by its primary key, you can use the `find` method:

```php
$cat = Cat::find(1);
```

Along with the `first` and `all` methods, there are **aggregate** methods. These allow you to retrieve aggregate values (rather than a record set) from your database tables:

```
use App\Order;

$orderCount    = Order::count();
$maximumTotal  = Order::max('amount');
$minimumTotal  = Order::min('amount');
$averageTotal  = Order::avg('amount');
$lifetimeSales = Order::sum('amount');
```

Filtering records

Eloquent also ships with a feature-rich query builder that allows you to build queries in code, without having to write a single line of SQL. This abstraction layer makes it easier to swap database platforms, should you ever need to. With Laravel, the only thing you need to do is update your database configuration and your application will continue to function as before.

Laravel's query builder has methods for common SQL-like directives such as WHERE, ORDER, and LIMIT; and more advanced concepts such as joins. For example, the previous `find` illustration can be expressed — albeit in longhand — as:

```
$cat = Cat::where('id', '=', 1)->first();
```

This will retrieve the first record WHERE `'id'` = 1. We will only expect one record when querying based on the primary key, so use the `first` method. If we have a more open WHERE clause, where we were expecting potentially more than one record, we can use the `get` method, as we did in the first code example, and it will only return records that matched that clause.

Clauses can also be **chained**. This allows you to build up complex query conditions by adding clauses together. Consider the following example code:

```
use App\User;

$users = User::where('gender', '=', 'Male')
  ->where('birth_date', '>', '1989-02-12')
  ->all();
```

This will find all male users who were born after February 12, 1989. Instead of specifying dates manually, we can also use **Carbon**, a date and time library. Here is an example of using Carbon to find all users who are older than 21 years of age:

```
use App\User;
use Carbon\Carbon;
```

```
$users = User::where('birth_date', '<', Carbon::now()- >subYears(21))
  ->all();
```

 You can find more information on Carbon and its available functions at its official GitHub repository `https://github.com/briannesbitt/Carbon`. Common Carbon methods are also covered in *Appendix, An Arsenal of Tools*.

Along with filtering records by WHERE conditions, you can also limit the number of records by using ranges using the `take` method:

```
$women = User::where('gender', '=', 'Female')->take(5)->get();
```

This will get the first five female users. You can also specify offsets by using the skip method:

```
$women = User::where('gender', '=', 'Female')->take(5)->
  skip(10)->get();
```

In SQL, this will look similar to the following:

```
SELECT * FROM users WHERE gender = 'Female' OFFSET 10 LIMIT 5
```

Queries can also be ordered by using the orderBy method:

```
$rankings = Team::orderBy('rating', 'asc')->get();
```

This will correspond to a SQL statement that looks like this:

```
SELECT * FROM teams ORDER BY rating ASC
```

Saving data

Applications that display data are great, but they're not very interactive. The fun comes when you allow users to submit data, whether these users are trusted contributors adding content via a content management system or contributions from general users on a site like Wikipedia.

When you retrieve a record via Eloquent, you can access its properties as follows:

```
$cat = Cat::find(1);
print $cat->name;
```

We can update attribute values in the same manner:

```
$cat->name = 'Garfield';
```

This will set the value in the model instance, but we need to persist the change to the database. We do this by calling the `save` method afterwards:

```
$cat->name = 'Garfield';
$cat->save();
```

If you have a table with lots of columns, then it will become tiresome to assign each property manually like this. To this end, Eloquent allows you to fill models by passing an associative array with values, and the keys representing the column names. You can fill a model while either creating or updating it:

```
$data = [
  'name' => 'Garfield',
  'birth_date' => '1978-06-19',
  'breed_id' => 1,
];

$cat->create($data);
```

However, this will throw a `MassAssignmentException` error.

Mass assignment

The preceding example is an example of **mass assignment**. That is where a model's attributes are blindly updated with values *en masse*. If the `$data` array in the previous example came from say, a user's form submission, then they can update any and all values in the same database.

Consider that you have a `users` table with a column called `is_admin`, which determines whether or not that user can view your website's administration area. Also consider that users on the public side of your website can update their profile. If, during form submission, the user also included a field with the name of `is_admin` and a value of `1`, that would update the column value in the database table and grant them access to your super secret admin area — this is a huge security concern and is exactly what mass-assignment protection prevents.

To mark columns whose values are safe to set via mass-assignment (such as `name`, `birth_date`, and so on.), we need to update our Eloquent models by providing a new property called `$fillable`. This is simply an array containing the names of the attributes that are safe to set via mass assignment:

```
class Cat extends Model {

  protected $table = 'cats';
  protected $fillable = [
    'name',
```

```
        'birth_date',
        'breed_id',
    ];
}
```

Now, we can create and update models by passing an array of data as before, without facing a `MassAssignmentException` being thrown.

Along with creating a new record, there are a couple of sibling methods that you can use. There is `firstOrCreate`, where you can pass an array of data—Eloquent will first try and find a model with the matching values. If it can't find a match, it will instead create the record.

There's also the similarly named `firstOrNew` method. However, instead of immediately saving the record to the database, it will instead just return a new Eloquent instance with the attribute values set, allowing you to set any other values first before manually saving it yourself.

A good time to use these methods is when allowing users to log in by using a third-party service such as Facebook or Twitter. These services will usually return information identifying the user, such as an e-mail address, allowing you to check your database for a matching user. If one exists, you can simply log them in, otherwise you can create a new user account for them.

Deleting data

There are two ways of deleting records. If you have a model instance that you have fetched from the database, then you can call the `delete` method on it:

```
$cat = Cat::find(1);
$cat->delete();
```

Alternatively, you can call the `destroy` method, specifying the IDs of the records you want to delete, without having to fetch those records first:

```
Cat::destroy(1);
Cat::destroy(1, 2, 3, 4, 5);
```

Soft deletion

By default, Eloquent will **hard-delete** records from your database. This means, once it's deleted, it's gone forever. If you need to retain deleted data (that is, for auditing), then you can use **soft deletes**. When deleting a model, the record is kept in the database but instead a `deleted_at` timestamp is set, and any records with this timestamp set will not be included when querying your database.

Soft deletes can be easily added to your Eloquent model. All you need to do is include the trait:

```
use Illuminate\Database\Eloquent\SoftDeletes;
class Cat extends Model {
  use SoftDeletes;
  protected $dates = ['deleted_at'];
}
```

We've also designated that the deleted_at column should be treated as a date column. This will yield the value as a Carbon instance and allow us to perform operations on it or display it in a variety of formats, should we need to.

You'll also need to make sure the deleted_at column is added to your table migration. An example of such a migration is as follows:

```
public function up() {
  $table->softDeletes();
}
```

Including deleted models in results

If you find you need to include deleted records when querying your database (for example, in an administration area), then you can use the withTrashed query scope. Query scopes are just methods you can use in chaining:

```
$cats = Cat::withTrashed()->get();
```

This will mix deleted records with non-deleted records. If you find you need to retrieve *only* deleted records, then you can use the onlyTrashed query scope:

```
$cats = Cat::onlyTrashed()->get();
```

If you find you need to "un-delete" a record, then the SoftDeletes trait provides you with a new restore method to undo this:

```
$cat->restore();
```

Finally, if you find you *really* need to delete a record from your database, you can use the forceDelete method. As the name implies, once you delete a record with this method, it's truly gone.

```
$cat->forceDelete();
```

Query scopes

The previous section introduced you to the concept of query scopes. This builds on from the query builder that allows you to build conditions on an ad hoc basis. However, what if you need certain conditions to apply to every request? Or a single condition that is actually the combination of multiple WHERE clauses? This is where query scopes come in.

Query scopes allow you to define these conditions once in your model, and then re-use them without having to manually define the clauses that make up that condition. For example, imagine we need to find users above the age of 21 in multiple places in our application. We can express this as a query scope:

```
class User extends Model {

  public function scopeOver21($query)
  {
    $date = Carbon::now()->subYears(21);
    return $query->where('birth_date', '<', $date);
  }
}
```

Thanks to the fluent query builder, we can now use this as follows:

```
$usersOver21 = User::over21()->get();
```

As you can see, query scopes are methods that begin with the word "scope", take the current query as a parameter, modify it in some way, and then return the modified query, ready to be used in another clause. This means you can chain query scopes just as you would any other query expression:

```
$malesOver21 = User::male()->over21()->get();
```

Along with simple scopes like these, we can create more "dynamic" scopes that accept parameters and can be passed to the scope's conditions. Consider the following example code:

```
class Cat extends Model {
  public function scopeOfBreed($query, $breedId)
  {
    return $query->where('breed_id', '=', $breedId);
  }
}
```

We can then find cats of a specific breed as follows:

```
$tabbyCats = Cat::ofBreed(1)->get();
```

Relationships

When we built our application in *Chapter 3, Your First Application*, we made use of relationships. Each cat in our application was of a particular breed. However, instead of storing the name of the breed next to every individual cat and potentially having the breed repeating numerous times, we created a separate `breeds` table and each cat's breed was a value that referred to the ID of a record in that table. This gave us an example of two types of relationships: a cat *belongs to* a breed, but a breed can *have many* cats. This is defined as a **one-to-many** relationship.

There are other types of relationships, for each of which Eloquent provides good support:

- One-to-one
- Many-to-many
- Has-many-through
- Polymorphic relations
- Many-to-many polymorphic relations

Here, we will look through them with an example of each.

One-to-one

Sometimes, you may want to split data across multiple tables for ease of management, or because they represent two different parts of one entity. A common example is a user, and a user's profile. You may have a `users` table that contains core information about that user such as their name, account e-mail address, and password hash; however, if it's a social networking website, then they may also have a profile with more information, such as their favorite color. This information can then be stored in a separate `profiles` table, with a foreign key representing the user that the profile belongs to.

In your models, this relation will look like this:

```
class User extends Model {

  public function profile()
  {
    return $this->hasOne('App\Profile');
  }
}
```

And in the `Profile` model, the relation will look like this:

```
class Profile extends Model {

  public function user()
  {
    return $this->belongsTo('App\User');
  }
}
```

When querying `Users`, we can also access their profile separately:

```
$profile = User::find(1)->profile;
```

Relations are accessed using the name of the method used to define it in the model. Since in the `User` model we defined the relation in a method called `profile`, this is the name of the property we use to access the data of that related model.

Many-to-many

A many-to-many relationship is more complicated than a one-to-one (where one model belongs to exactly one other model) or a one-to-many relationship (where many models can belong to one other model). As the name suggests, many models can belong to many other models. To accomplish this, instead of just two tables being involved, a third is introduced. This can be quite difficult to comprehend, so let's look at an example.

Imagine you're building a permissions system to limit what actions each user can perform. Instead of assigning permissions on a per-user basis, you instead have roles, where each user is given a subset of permissions, depending on which role they've been assigned. In this description, we've identified two entities: a `User` and a `Role`. Also in this scenario, a user can have many roles, and a role can belong to many users. To map roles to users, we create a third table, called a join table. Laravel refers to these tables as **pivot** tables, a term you may have heard of if you have worked with spreadsheets before.

By default, Eloquent expects join tables to contain the singular names of the two target tables, listed alphabetically and separated by an underscore. So in our scenario, this would be `role_user`. The table itself contains only two columns (other than the primary key). These columns represent the foreign key of the `Role` model and the `User` model it is creating a relation between. Again in convention over configuration, these should be lowercase, singular, with `_id` appended, that is, `role_id` and `user_id`.

The relationship is defined in both our `User` and `Role` models using the `belongsToMany` method:

```
class User extends Model {
  public function roles()
  {
    return $this->belongsToMany('App\Role');
  }
}

class Role extends Model {
  public function users()
  {
    return $this->belongsToMany('App\User');
  }
}
```

We can now find out what roles a user has been assigned:

```
$roles = User::find(1)->roles;
```

We can also find out all users with a particular role:

```
$admins = Role::find(1)->users;
```

If you need to add a new role to a user, you can do so by using the `attach` method:

```
$user = User::find(1);
$user->roles()->attach($roleId);
```

And, of course, the opposite of `attach` is `detach`:

```
$user->roles()->detach($roleId);
```

Both the `attach` and `detach` methods also accept arrays, allowing you to add/ remove multiple relations in one operation.

Alternatively, you can use the `sync` method. The difference with `sync` is, only after the operation is complete are the IDs that are passed present in the join table, rather than adding/removing them from the existing relations.

```
$user->roles()->sync(1, 2, 3, 4, 5);
```

Storing data in the pivot table

Along with storing the primary keys of both the related models in the pivot table, you can also store additional data. Imagine we have users and groups in an application. Many users can belong to many groups, but users can also be moderators of groups. To indicate which users are moderators of a group, we can add a `is_moderator` column on the pivot table. To specify the additional data that should be stored in the pivot table, we can specify a second parameter when calling the `attach` method:

```
$user->groups()->attach(1, ['is_moderator' => true]);
```

We can use the same approach when using the `sync` method too:

```
$user->groups()->sync([1 => ['is_moderator' => true]]);
```

Has-many-through

With related data, things are simple when you want data from a model that is directly related to the current one you're working with; but what happens if you want data that is two **hops** away from your current model?

Consider a simple e-commerce website. You may have a `Product` model, an `Order` model, and an `OrderItem` model that belongs to both a product and an order. You have been tasked with finding all orders that contain a particular product. How do you do this if `Product` isn't directly associated with `Order`? Thankfully, in our scenario, they have a common relation—the `OrderItem` model.

We can use a "has-many-through" relationship to reach orders a product is part of via the intermediate `OrderItem` model. We set the relationship up in our `Product` model, as follows:

```
class Product extends Model {

  public function orders()
  {
    return $this->hasManyThrough('App\Order', 'App\OrderItem');
  }
}
```

The first parameter in the `hasManyThrough` method is the target model, and the second parameter is the intermediate model we go through to get to it. We can now easily list the orders a product is part of:

```
$product = Product::find(1);
$orders = $product->orders;
```

Polymorphic relations

Polymorphic relations are difficult to grasp at first; however, once you have an understanding of them, they are really powerful. They allow a model to belong to more than one other model on a single association.

A common use case for a polymorphic relationship is to create an image library and then allow your other models to contain images by linking to the relevant records in the image library table. A base `Image` model will look like this:

```
class Image extends Model {

  public function imageable()
  {
    return $this->morphTo();
  }
}
```

The `morphTo` method is what makes this model polymorphic. Now, in our other models, we can create a relation to the `Image` model, as follows:

```
class Article extends Model {
  public function images()
  {
    $this->morphMany('App\Image', 'imageable');
  }
}
```

You can now fetch any related `Image` models through your `Article` model:

```
$article = Article::find(1);

foreach ($article->images as $image) {
  // Do something with image
}
```

You may think that this is no different to a one-to-many relationship, but the difference becomes apparent when you look at the relation from the other side. When retrieving an `Image` instance, if you access the `imageable` relation, you'll receive an instance of whatever model "owns" the image. This may be an `Article`, a `Product`, or another model type in your application. Eloquent achieves this by not only storing a foreign key value, but also the name of the model class. In the case of our `Image` model, the columns would be `imageable_id` and `imageable_type`. When creating your migration, there is a method to create these two columns:

```
$table->morphs('imageable');
```

Many-to-many polymorphic relations

The final relation type we will look at is the **many-to-many polymorphic relation**, by far the most complex. Staying with our image library example, we can see that it has one drawback, an `Image` can only belong to one other model at a time. So, while we can see all images that have been uploaded by models in our application, we can't re-use an uploaded image like we would in a true image library. This is where a many-to-many polymorphic relation would come in.

Keeping our `images` and `articles` tables, we need to introduce a third table, `imageables`. The relation data is removed from the `images` table, and instead placed in this new table, which also has another column that is a foreign key pointing to the `Image` primary key. The three columns are:

- `image_id`
- `imageable_id`
- `imageable_type`

With this schema, a single `Image` can have multiple relations. That is, the image can be re-used in multiple models, whether that is multiple `Article` records, or models of different types. Our updated model classes then take this form:

```
class Article extends Model {
  public function images()
  {
    return $this->morphedByMany('App\Image', 'imageable');
  }
}
```

The `Image` model is also updated, containing methods for each of its relationships:

```
class Image extends Model {
  public function articles()
  {
    return $this->morphToMany('App\Article', 'imageable');
  }
  public function products()
  {
    return $this->morphToMany('App\Product', 'imageable');
  }
  // And any other relations
}
```

You can still access the `images` relation as with a normal polymorphic relationship.

Model events

Eloquent fires numerous events at different points, such as when a model is being saved or deleted. The following is a list of methods Eloquent models can fire:

- `creating`
- `created`
- `updating`
- `updated`
- `saving`
- `saved`
- `deleting`
- `deleted`
- `restoring`
- `restored`

The names are self-explanatory. The difference in the past and present participles is that events such as `creating` are fired *before* the model is created, whereas `created` is fired *after* the model has been created. Therefore, if you were to halt execution within a handler for the `creating` event, the record will not be saved; whereas, if you halted execution within a handler for the `created` event, the record would still be persisted to the database.

Registering event listeners

It's quite open-ended as to where to register listeners for model events. One place is in the `boot` method within the `EventServiceProvider` class:

```
public function boot(DispatcherContract $events)
{
  parent::boot($events);

  User::creating(function($user)
  {
    // Do something
  });
}
```

Be sure to import the namespace for the `DispatcherContract` at the top of the file:

```
use Illuminate\Contracts\Bus\Dispatcher as DispatcherContract;
```

Eloquent models provide a method for each event that you can pass an anonymous function to. This anonymous function receives an instance of the model that you can then act upon. So if you wanted to create a URL-friendly representation of an article headline each time your `Article` model was saved, you can do this by listening on the saving event:

```
Article::saving(function($article)
{
    $article->slug = Str::slug($article->headline);
});
```

Model observers

As you add more and more model event handlers to your `EventServiceProvider` class, you may find it becoming overcrowded and difficult to maintain. This is where an alternative to handling model events comes into play — model observers.

Model observers are standalone classes that you attach to a model, and implement methods for as many events as you need to listen out for. So our slug-creating function can be re-factored into a model observer as follows:

```
use Illuminate\Support\Str;

class ArticleObserver {
    public function saving($article)
    {
        $article->slug = Str::slug($article->headline);
    }
}
```

We can then register our observer in our `EventServiceProvider` class:

```
public function boot(DispatcherContract $events)
{
    parent::boot($events);
    Article::observe(new ArticleObserver);
}
```

Collections

Historically, other frameworks that have shipped with their own ORMs and query builders have returned result sets as either multidimensional arrays or **Plain Old PHP Objects (POPOs)**. Eloquent has taken its cue from other, more mature ORMs and instead returns result sets as an instance of a collection object.

The collection object is powerful as it not only contains the data returned from the database, but also many helper methods, allowing you to manipulate that data before displaying it to the user.

Checking whether a key exists in a collection

If you need to find out whether a particular key exists in a collection, you can use the `contains` method:

```
$users = User::all();
if ($users->contains($userId))
{
  // Do something
}
```

When querying models, any relations are also returned as subcollections, allowing you to use the exact same methods on relations too:

```
$user = User::find(1);
if ($user->roles->contains($roleId))
{
  // Do something
}
```

By default, models return an instance of `Illuminate\Database\Eloquent\Collection`. However, this can be overridden to instead use a different class. This is handy if we wanted to add additional methods to collections.

Say for a collection of roles and we want to determine if administrator is one of those roles. If we imagine the administrator role to have a primary key value of `1`, we can create a new method, like this:

```
<?php namespace App;
use Illuminate\Database\Eloquent\Collection as EloquentCollection;
class RoleCollection extends EloquentCollection {
  public function containsAdmin()
  {
    return $this->contains(1);
  }
}
```

The second part is to then tell the `Role` model to use our new collection:

```
use App\RoleCollection;

class Role extends Model {
```

```
    public function newCollection(array $models = array())
    {
        return new RoleCollection($models);
    }
}
```

Instead of instantiating the default Eloquent collection, it will instead create a new instance of our `RoleCollection` class, filling it with the results from our query. This means that every time we request roles, we can use our new `containsAdmin` method:

```
$user = User::find(1);

if ($user->roles->containsAdmin())
{
    // Let user administrate something
}
else
{
    // User does not have administrator role
}
```

Eloquent collections also have a plethora of other helpful functions for allowing you to manipulate, filter, and iterate over items. You can view more information on these methods at `http://laravel.com/docs/master/eloquent#collections`.

Summary

Although we have covered a lot in this chapter, Eloquent is so feature-rich that unfortunately, there isn't room to cover each and every one of its features. We have covered the most important aspects of Eloquent, though, and that will set you well on your way to saving and retrieving data, creating relations of varying complexity between your models, and handling various events raised during your models' lifecycle.

The next chapter sees us move on to learn all about testing our application so it remains as bulletproof as possible.

5
Testing – It's Easier Than You Think

Testing is an often-neglected part in PHP development. Compared to languages such as Java and Ruby, where testing is strongly ingrained into the workflow of developers, PHP has been lagging behind. This is mainly because simple PHP applications tend to be tightly coupled and are, therefore, difficult to test. However, thanks to standardization and modularization efforts and frameworks that encourage the separation of concerns, PHP testing has become more accessible and the mentality towards it is slowly changing.

Laravel 5 is a framework that was built from the ground up to facilitate testing. It comes with all the necessary files to get started, along with different helpers to test your application, thus helping beginners to overcome some of the biggest obstacles.

In this chapter, we will demonstrate how Laravel makes it very simple to get started with testing, without forcing you to go for a test-first approach, or making you aim for complete test coverage. In this gentle introduction to testing, we will look at the following topics:

- The advantages of writing tests for your application
- How to prepare your tests
- The software design patterns that Laravel fosters
- How to use Mockery to test objects in isolation
- The built-in features and helpers that facilitate testing

The benefits of testing

If you have not written tests for your web applications before, the advantages of testing might not always be obvious to you. After all, preparing and writing tests involves significant time investment, and for short-lived prototypes or hackathon projects, they can even seem to be a complete waste of time. However, in almost all the other cases, when your project is likely to grow in complexity, or when you collaborate with other developers, tests have the potential to save you and other people a lot of time and headaches.

Tests also introduce some changes to your workflow. In the development stage, you will no longer have to switch back and forth between your code editor and your web browser. Instead, if you are using a text editor or an IDE that supports it, you could bind a test runner to a keyboard shortcut.

Once you have proven that a certain bit of functionality works, you will have a way of quickly ensuring that it continues to work as expected, if the source code is changed at a later date. In addition to this, it forces you to clearly and unambiguously define the expected behavior of your application and can therefore complement or replace a significant part of the documentation. This can be particularly helpful, not only for new developers who start collaborating on the project, but also for yourself, if you have not touched the project for a while.

The anatomy of a test

Your application tests will reside in `tests/`. In this directory, you will find a base test case inside `TestCase.php`, which is responsible for bootstrapping the application in the testing environment. This class extends Laravel's main `TestCase` class, which in turn extends the `PHPUnit_Framework_TestCase` class, along with many helpful testing methods that we will cover later in this chapter. All of your tests will extend this first `TestCase` class and define one or more methods that are meant to test one or more features of your application.

In every test, we generally perform the following three distinct tasks:

1. We *arrange* or initialize some data.
2. We execute a function to *act* on this data.
3. We *assert* or verify that the output matches what we expected.

Given we had the following Helper class:

```
class Helper {
  public static function sum($arr) { return array_sum($arr); }
}
```

An example test case, `HelperTest.php`, which illustrates the three preceding steps, will look like this:

```php
class HelperTest extends PHPUnit_Framework_TestCase {
  public function testSum() {
    $data = [1,2,3];                    // 1) Arrange
    $result = Helper::sum($data);       // 2) Act
    $this->assertEquals(6, $result);    // 3) Assert
  }
  public function testSomethingElse() {
    // ...
  }
}
```

When the preceding code snippet is executed, PHPUnit will run each method within the test case and keep track of how many tests failed or passed. With PHPUnit installed on your system, you can run this test, using the following command:

```
$ phpunit --colors HelperTest.php
```

This will produce the following output:

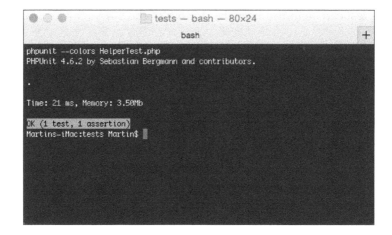

 Most code editors also provide ways to run this directly within the editor by pressing a shortcut key. Examples of such editors include **PhpStorm**. It is even possible to run them automatically before each commit or before you deploy your code to a remote server.

Unit testing with PHPUnit

A positive effect of testing is that it forces you to split your code into manageable dependencies, so that you can test them in isolation. The testing of these individual classes and methods is referred to as **unit testing**. Since it relies on the PHPUnit testing framework, which already provides a large number of tools to set up test suites, Laravel does not need to provide any additional helpers for this type of testing.

A great way to learn about any framework, and at the same time learn about the different ways in which it can be tested, is to look at how its authors have written tests for it. Therefore, our next examples will be taken directly from Laravel's test suite, which is located at `vendor/laravel/framework/tests/`.

Defining what you expect with assertions

Assertions are the fundamental components of unit tests. Simply put, they are used to compare the *expected output* of a function with its *actual output*.

To see how assertions work, we will examine the test for the `Str::is()` helper, which checks whether a given string matches a given pattern.

The following test can be found near the bottom of the `Support/SupportStrTest.php` file:

```php
use Illuminate\Support\Str;
class SupportStrTest extends PHPUnit_Framework_TestCase {
  // ...
  public function testIs()
  {
    $this->assertTrue(Str::is('/', '/'));
    $this->assertFalse(Str::is('/', ' /'));
    $this->assertFalse(Str::is('/', '/a'));
    $this->assertTrue(Str::is('foo/*', 'foo/bar/baz'));
    $this->assertTrue(Str::is('*/foo', 'blah/baz/foo'));
  }
}
```

The preceding test performs five assertions to test whether the method is indeed returning the expected value when called with different parameters.

PHPUnit provides many other assertion methods that can, for example, help you test for numerical values with `assertGreaterThan()`, equality with `assertEquals()`, types with `assertInstanceOf()`, or existence with `assertArrayHasKey()`. While there are many more possible assertions, these are the ones you will probably end up using most frequently. In total, PHPUnit provides around 40 different assertion methods, all of which are described in the official documentation at `http://phpunit.de/manual/`.

Preparing the scene and cleaning up objects

If you need to run a function before each test method to set up some test data or reduce code duplication, you can use the `setUp()` method. If, on the other hand, you need to run some code after each test to clear any objects that were instantiated in your tests, you can define it inside the `tearDown()` method. A good example would be to remove any records from a database inserted in the `setUp()` method.

Expecting exceptions

It is also possible to test for exceptions by decorating your function with an `@expectedException` DocBlock, like Laravel does inside `Database/DatabaseEloquentModelTest.php`:

```
/**
 * @expectedException Illuminate\Database\Eloquent\
MassAssignmentException
 */
public function testGlobalGuarded()
{
  $model = new EloquentModelStub;
  $model->guard(['*']);
  $model->fill(['name' => 'foo', 'age' => 'bar',
    'votes' => 'baz']);
}
```

In this test function, there is no assertion, but the code is expected to throw an exception when it is executed. Also note the use of an `EloquentModelStub` object. A stub creates an instance of an object that provides or simulates the methods that our class needs—in this case, an Eloquent model on which we can call the `guard()` and `fill()` methods. If you look at the definition of this stub further down in the test, you will see that it does not actually interact with a database, but it provides canned responses instead.

Testing interdependent classes in isolation

In addition to stubs, which we looked at in the previous section, there is another way in which you can test one or more interdependent classes in isolation. It is by using **mocks**. In Laravel, mocks are created using the Mockery library, and they help define the methods that should be called during the test, the arguments they should receive, and their return values as well. Laravel heavily relies on mocks in its own tests. An example can be found in the AuthEloquentUserProviderTest class, where the Hasher class is mocked:

```
use Mockery as M;

class AuthEloquentUserProviderTest extends
  PHPUnit_Framework_TestCase {

  public function tearDown(){
    M::close();
  }
  // ...

  public function getProviderMock() {
    $hasher = m::mock('Illuminate\Contracts\Hashing\Hasher');
    return $this->getMock('Illuminate\Auth\EloquentUserProvider',
      array('createModel'), array($hasher, 'foo'));
  }
}
```

As opposed to stubs, mocks allow us to define which methods need to be called, how many times they should be called, which parameters they should receive, and which parameters they should return. If any of these preconditions are not met, the test will fail.

To ensure that we do not have an instance of a mocked object that persists and interferes with future tests, Mockery provides a close() method that needs to be executed after each test. Thanks to this mock, the class can be tested in complete isolation.

End-to-end testing

When we are confident that all of the interdependent classes work as expected, we can then conduct another type of testing. It consists of simulating the kind of interaction that a user would have through a web browser. This user would, for example, visit a specific URL, perform certain actions, and expect to see some kind of feedback from the application.

This is perhaps the most straightforward type of testing, as it mimics the kind of testing that you manually perform each time you refresh your browser after a code change. When you get started, it is absolutely fine to only perform this type of testing. However, you must bear in mind that if any errors occur, you will still have to drill deep down into your code to find the exact component that caused the error.

Testing – batteries included

When you start a new project with Laravel, you are provided with both a configuration file with sensible defaults for PHPUnit at the root of the project inside `phpunit.xml` as well as a directory, `tests/`, where you are expected to save your tests. This directory even contains an example test that you can use as a starting point.

With these settings in place, from the root of our project, all we need to do is SSH into our Homestead virtual machine and run the following command:

```
$ phpunit
```

This command will read the XML configuration file and run our tests. If, at this stage, you get an error message telling you that PHPUnit cannot be found, you either need to add the `phpunit` command to your `PATH` variable or install it with Composer.

Laravel applications come with PHPUnit already declared in the `autoload-dev` block in your `composer.json` file. After running `composer update`, you will be able to call PHPUnit by using the following command:

```
$ vendor/bin/phpunit
```

Framework assertions

Now that we know about the two major types of tests and have PHPUnit installed, we are going to write a few tests for the application that we developed in *Chapter 3, Your First Application*.

This first test will verify whether visitors are redirected to the correct page when they first visit our site:

```
public function testHomePageRedirection() {
  $this->call('GET', '/');
  $this->assertRedirectedTo('cats');
}
```

Here, we made use of the call() method that simulated a request to our application, which executes the request through Laravel's HTTP kernel. Then, we used one of the assertion methods provided by Laravel to make sure that the response is a redirection to the new location. If you now run the phpunit command, you should see the following output:

```
OK (1 test, 2 assertions)
```

Next, we can try to write a test to make sure that the creation form is not accessible to the users that are not logged in; this is shown in the following code snippet:

```
public function testGuestIsRedirected() {
  $this->call('GET', '/cats/create');
  $this->assertRedirectedTo('login');
}'
```

Impersonating users

Sometimes, you may wish to run a test as if you were a registered user of the application. This is possible by using the be() method and passing a User instance to it or whichever Eloquent model you use, along with Laravel's authentication class:

```
public function testLoggedInUserCanCreateCat() {
  $user = new App\User([
    'name' => 'John Doe',
    'is_admin' => false,
  ]);
  $this->be($user);
  $this->call('GET', '/cats/create');
  $this->assertResponseOk();
}
```

Testing with a database

While some developers would advise against writing tests that hit the database, it can often be a simple and effective way of making sure that all the components work together as expected. However, it should only be done once each individual unit has been tested. Let's also not forget that Laravel has support for migrations and seeding; in other words, it has all of the tools that are required to recreate an identical data structure from scratch, before each test.

To write tests that depend on a database, we need to override the setUp() method in our tests to migrate and seed the database each time a test is run. It is also important to run the parent setUp() method, otherwise, the test case will not be able to start properly:

```
public function setUp(){
  parent::setUp();
  Artisan::call('migrate');
  $this->seed();
}
```

Then, we need to configure a test database connection in `config/database.php`; if the application does not contain any database-specific queries, we can use SQLite's in-memory feature by setting `:memory:` instead of a path to the database file. The following configuration also has the potential to speed up our tests:

```
'sqlite' => [
  'driver'   => 'sqlite',
  'database' => ':memory:',
],
```

And lastly, since we are going to test the editing and deletion features, we are going to need at least one row in the `cats` table of our database, so we prepare a seeder that will insert a cat with a forced `id` of value `1`:

```
class CatsTableSeeder extends Seeder {
  public function run(){
    Cat::create(['id' => 1, 'name' => '''Tom', 'user_id' => 1]);
  }
}
```

Once this is done, we can test the deletion feature as follows:

```
public function testOwnerCanDeleteCat() {
  $user = new App\User(['id' => 1, 'name' => 'User #1',
    'is_admin' => false]);
  $this->be($user);
  $this->call('DELETE', '/cats/1');
  $this->assertRedirectedTo('/cats');
  $this->assertSessionHas('message');
}
```

Note that this time, we did not need to enable the filters since the permissions are checked by a method in the `User` model. Since the database is wiped and re-seeded after each test, we do not need to worry about the fact that the previous test deleted that particular cat. We can also write a test to ensure that a user who is not an administrator cannot edit someone else's cat profile:

```
public function testNonAdminCannotEditCat() {
  $user = new App\User(['id' => 2, 'name' => 'User #2',
    'is_admin' => false]);
  $this->be($user);
  $this->call('DELETE', '/cats/1');
```

```
    $this->assertRedirectedTo('/cats/1');
    $this->assertSessionHas('error');
}
```

Inspecting the rendered views

Since Laravel ships with Symfony's `DomCrawler` and `CssSelector` components, it is possible to inspect the contents of a rendered view. By issuing a request through the test client instance with `$this->client->request()`, you can filter its contents with CSS queries as follows:

```
public function testAdminCanEditCat() {
    $user = new App\User(['id' => 3, 'name' => 'Admin',
      'is_admin' => true));
    $this->be($user);
    $newName = 'Berlioz';
    $this->call('PUT', '/cats/1', ['name' => $newName]);
    $crawler = $this->client->request('GET', '/cats/1');
    $this->assertCount(1, $crawler
      ->filter('h2:contains("'.$newName.'")'));
}
```

The complete documentation for the `DomCrawler` component can be found at `http://symfony.com/doc/current/components/dom_crawler.html`. If you are already familiar with jQuery, its syntax will look familiar to you.

Summary

While the main ideas behind testing are easy to grasp, it is often their implementation that can prove to be an obstacle, especially when working with a new framework. However, after reading this chapter, you should have a good overview of how you can test your Laravel applications. The techniques presented in this chapter will enable you to write more robust and future-proof applications.

In the next chapter, we will explore the possibilities offered by Artisan, Laravel's command-line utility.

6

A Command-line Companion
Called Artisan

In the last few chapters, we have used Artisan for various tasks, such as running database migrations. However, as we will see in this chapter, Laravel's command-line utility has far more capabilities and can be used to run and automate all sorts of tasks. In the next pages, you will learn how Artisan can help you:

- Inspect and interact with your application
- Enhance the overall performance of your application
- Write your own commands

By the end of this tour of Artisan's capabilities, you will understand how it can become an indispensable companion in your projects.

Keeping up with the latest changes

New features are constantly being added to Laravel. If a few days have passed since you first installed it, try running a `composer update` command from your terminal. You should see the latest versions of Laravel and its dependencies being downloaded. Since you are already in the terminal, finding out about the latest features is just one command away:

```
$ php artisan changes
```

This saves you from going online to find a change log or reading through a long history of commits on GitHub. It can also help you learn about features that you were not aware of. You can also find out which version of Laravel you are running by entering the following command:

```
$ php artisan --version
Laravel Framework version 5.0.16
```

All Artisan commands have to be run from your project's root directory.

 With the help of a short script such as Artisan Anywhere, available at `https://github.com/antonioribeiro/artisan-anywhere`, it is also possible to run Artisan from any subfolder in your project.

Inspecting and interacting with your application

With the `route:list` command, you can see at a glance which URLs your application will respond to, what their names are, and if any middleware has been registered to handle requests. This is probably the quickest way to get acquainted with a Laravel application that someone else has built.

To display a table with all the routes, all you have to do is enter the following command:

```
$ php artisan route:list
```

For example, the following is what the application we built in *Chapter 3, Your First Application*, looks like:

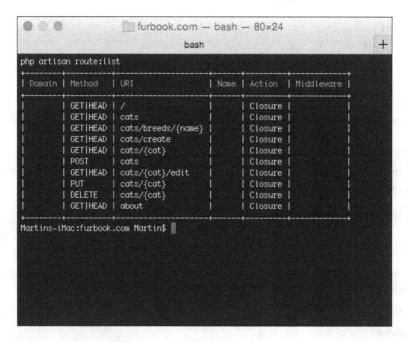

In some applications, you might see /{v1}/{v2}/{v3}/{v4}/ {v5} appended to particular routes. This is because the developer has registered a controller with implicit routing, and Laravel will try to match and pass up to five parameters to the controller.

Fiddling with the internals

When developing your application, you will sometimes need to run short, one-off commands to inspect the contents of your database, insert some data into it, or check the syntax and results of an Eloquent query. One way you could do this is by creating a temporary route with a closure that is going to trigger these actions. However, this is less than practical since it requires you to switch back and forth between your code editor and your web browser.

To make these small changes easier, Artisan provides a command called `tinker`, which boots up the application and lets you interact with it. Just enter the following command:

```
$ php artisan tinker
```

This will start a **Read-Eval-Print Loop** (**REPL**) similar to what you get when running the `php -a` command, which starts an interactive shell. In this REPL, you can enter PHP commands in the context of the application and immediately see their output:

```
> $cat = 'Garfield';
> App\Cat::create(['name' => $cat,'date_of_birth' => new DateTime]);
> echo App\Cat::whereName($cat)->get();
[{"id":"4","name":"Garfield 2","date_of_birth":…}]
> dd(Config::get('database.default'));
```

Version 5 of Laravel leverages PsySH, a PHP-specific REPL that provides a more robust shell with support for keyboard shortcuts and history.

Turning the engine off

Whether it is because you are upgrading a database or waiting to push a fix for a critical bug to production, you may want to manually put your application on hold to avoid serving a broken page to your visitors. You can do this by entering the following command:

```
$ php artisan down
```

This will put your application into **maintenance** mode. You can determine what to display to users when they visit your application in this mode by editing the template file at `resources/views/errors/503.blade.php` (since maintenance mode sends an HTTP status code of `503 Service Unavailable` to the client). To exit maintenance mode, simply run the following command:

```
$ php artisan up
```

Fine-tuning your application

For every incoming request, Laravel has to load many different classes and this can slow down your application, particularly if you are not using a PHP accelerator such as **APC**, **eAccelerator**, or **XCache**. In order to reduce disk I/O and shave off precious milliseconds from each request, you can run the following command:

```
$ php artisan optimize
```

This will trim and merge many common classes into one file located inside `storage/framework/compiled.php`. The `optimize` command is something you could, for example, include in a deployment script.

By default, Laravel will not compile your classes if `app.debug` is set to `true`. You can override this by adding the `--force` flag to the command but bear in mind that this will make your error messages less readable.

Caching routes

Apart from caching class maps to improve the response time of your application, you can also cache the routes of your application. This is something else you can include in your deployment process. The command? Simply enter the following:

```
$ php artisan route:cache
```

The advantage of caching routes is that your application will get a little faster as its routes will have been pre-compiled, instead of evaluating the URL and any matches routes on each request. However, as the routing process now refers to a cache file, any new routes added will not be parsed. You will need to re-cache them by running the `route:cache` command again. Therefore, this is not suitable during development, where routes might be changing frequently.

Generators

Laravel 5 ships with various commands to generate new files of different types. Throughout the book, we've already used a couple (that is, for generating new migration files), but there are others too. If you run `$ php artisan list` under the `make` namespace, you will find the following entries:

- `make:command`
- `make:console`
- `make:controller`
- `make:event`
- `make:middleware`
- `make:migration`
- `make:model`
- `make:provider`
- `make:request`

These commands create a stub file in the appropriate location in your Laravel application containing boilerplate code ready for you to get started with. This saves keystrokes, creating these files from scratch. All of these commands require a name to be specified, as shown in the following command:

$ php artisan make:model Cat

This will create an Eloquent model class called `Cat` at `app/Cat.php`, as well as a corresponding migration to create a `cats` table. If you do not need to create a migration when making a model (for example, if the table already exists), then you can pass the `--no-migration` option as follows:

$ php artisan make:model Cat --no-migration

A new model class will look like this:

```php
<?php namespace App;
use Illuminate\Database\Eloquent\Model;
class Cat extends Model {
  //
}
```

From here, you can define your own properties and methods.

The other commands may have options. The best way to check is to append `--help` after the command name, as shown in the following command:

```
$ php artisan make:command --help
```

You will see that this command has `--handler` and `--queued` options to modify the class stub that is created.

Rolling out your own Artisan commands

At this stage you might be thinking about writing your own bespoke commands. As you will see, this is surprisingly easy to do with Artisan. If you have used Symfony's Console component, you will be pleased to know that an Artisan command is simply an extension of it with a slightly more expressive syntax. This means the various helpers will prompt for input, show a progress bar, or format a table, are all available from within Artisan.

The command that we are going to write depends on the application we built in *Chapter 3, Your First Application*. It will allow you to export all cat records present in the database as a CSV with or without a header line. If no output file is specified, the command will simply dump all records onto the screen in a formatted table.

Creating the command

There are only two required steps to create a command. Firstly, you need to create the command itself, and then you need to register it manually.

We can make use of the following command to create a console command we have seen previously:

```
$ php artisan make:console ExportCatsCommand
```

This will generate a class inside `app/Console/Commands`. We will then need to register this command with the console kernel, located at `app/Console/Kernel.php`:

```
protected $commands = [
  'App\Console\Commands\ExportCatsCommand',
];
```

If you now run `php artisan`, you should see a new command called `command:name`. This command does not do anything yet. However, before we start writing the functionality, let's briefly look at how it works internally.

The anatomy of a command

Inside the newly created command class, you will find some code that has been generated for you. We will walk through the different properties and methods and see what their purpose is.

The first two properties are the name and description of the command. Nothing exciting here, this is only the information that will be shown in the command line when you run Artisan. The colon is used to namespace the commands, as shown here:

```
protected $name = 'export:cats';

protected $description = 'Export all cats';
```

Then you will find the `fire` method. This is the method that gets called when you run a particular command. From there, you can retrieve the arguments and options passed to the command, or run other methods.

```
public function fire()
```

Lastly, there are two methods that are responsible for defining the list of arguments or options that are passed to the command:

```
protected function getArguments() { /* Array of arguments */ }
protected function getOptions() { /* Array of options */ }
```

Each argument or option can have a name, a description, and a default value that can be mandatory or optional. Additionally, options can have a shortcut.

To understand the difference between arguments and options, consider the following command, where options are prefixed with two dashes:

```
$ command --option_one=value --option_two -v=1 argument_one
  argument_two
```

In this example, `option_two` does not have a value; it is only used as a flag. The `-v` flag only has one dash since it is a shortcut. In your console commands, you'll need to verify any option and argument values the user provides (for example, if you're expecting a number, to ensure the value passed is actually a numerical value).

Arguments can be retrieved with `$this->argument($arg)`, and options — you guessed it — with `$this->option($opt)`. If these methods do not receive any parameters, they simply return the full list of parameters. You refer to arguments and options via their names, that is, `$this->argument('argument_name');`.

Writing the command

We are going to start by writing a method that retrieves all cats from the database and returns them as an array:

```
protected function getCatsData() {
    $cats = App\Cat::with('breed')->get();
    foreach ($cats as $cat) {
        $output[] = [
            $cat->name,
            $cat->date_of_birth,
            $cat->breed->name,
        ];
    }
    return $output;
}
```

There should not be anything new here. We could have used the `toArray()` method, which turns an Eloquent collection into an array, but we would have had to flatten the array and exclude certain fields.

Then we need to define what arguments and options our command expects:

```
protected function getArguments() {
    return [
        ['file', InputArgument::OPTIONAL, 'The output file', null],
    ];
}
```

To specify additional arguments, just add an additional element to the array with the same parameters:

```
return [
    ['arg_one', InputArgument::OPTIONAL, 'Argument 1', null],
    ['arg_two', InputArgument::OPTIONAL, 'Argument 2', null],
];
```

The options are defined in a similar way:

```
protected function getOptions() {
    return [
        ['headers', 'h', InputOption::VALUE_NONE, 'Display headers?',
        null],
    ];
}
```

The last parameter is the default value that the argument and option should have if it is not specified. In both the cases, we want it to be `null`.

Lastly, we write the logic for the `fire` method:

```
public function fire() {
  $output_path = $this->argument('file');

  $headers = ['Name', 'Date of Birth', 'Breed'];
  $rows = $this->getCatsData();

  if ($output_path) {
    $handle = fopen($output_path, 'w');
      if ($this->option('headers')) {
        fputcsv($handle, $headers);
      }
      foreach ($rows as $row) {
        fputcsv($handle, $row);
      }
      fclose($handle);

  } else {
        $table = $this->getHelperSet()->get('table');
        $table->setHeaders($headers)->setRows($rows);
        $table->render($this->getOutput());
    }
}
```

While the bulk of this method is relatively straightforward, there are a few novelties. The first one is the use of the `$this->info()` method, which writes an informative message to the output. If you need to show an error message in a different color, you can use the `$this->error()` method.

Further down in the code, you will see some functions that are used to generate a table. As we mentioned previously, an Artisan command extends the Symfony console component and, therefore, inherits all of its helpers. These can be accessed with `$this->getHelperSet()`. Then it is only a matter of passing arrays for the header and rows of the table, and calling the `render` method.

To see the output of our command, we will run the following command:

```
$ php artisan export:cats
$ php artisan export:cats --headers file.csv
```

Scheduling commands

Traditionally, if you wanted a command to run periodically (hourly, daily, weekly, and so on), then you would have to set up a Cron job in Linux-based environments, or a scheduled task in Windows environments. However, this comes with drawbacks. It requires the user to have server access and familiarity with creating such schedules. Also, in cloud-based environments, the application may not be hosted on a single machine, or the user might not have the privileges to create Cron jobs. The creators of Laravel saw this as something that could be improved, and have come up with an expressive way of scheduling Artisan tasks.

Your schedule is defined in `app/Console/Kernel.php`, and with your schedule being defined in this file, it has the added advantage of being present in source control.

If you open the Kernel class file, you will see a method named `schedule`. Laravel ships with one by default that serves as an example:

```
$schedule->command('inspire')->hourly();
```

If you've set up a Cron job in the past, you will see that this is instantly more readable than the crontab equivalent:

```
0 * * * * /path/to/artisan inspire
```

Specifying the task in code also means we can easily change the console command to be run without having to update the crontab entry.

By default, scheduled commands will not run. To do so, you need a single Cron job that runs the scheduler each and every minute:

```
* * * * * php /path/to/artisan schedule:run 1>> /dev/null 2>&1
```

When the scheduler is run, it will check for any jobs whose schedules match and then runs them. If no schedules match, then no commands are run in that pass.

You are free to schedule as many commands as you wish, and there are various methods to schedule them that are expressive and descriptive:

```
$schedule->command('foo')->everyFiveMinutes();
$schedule->command('bar')->everyTenMinutes();
$schedule->command('baz')->everyThirtyMinutes();
$schedule->command('qux')->daily();
```

You can also specify a time for a scheduled command to run:

```
$schedule->command('foo')->dailyAt('21:00');
```

Alternatively, you can create less frequent scheduled commands:

```
$schedule->command('foo')->weekly();
$schedule->command('bar')->weeklyOn(1, '21:00');
```

The first parameter in the second example is the day, with 0 representing Sunday, and 1 through 6 representing Monday through Saturday, and the second parameter is the time, again specified in 24-hour format. You can also explicitly specify the day on which to run a scheduled command:

```
$schedule->command('foo')->mondays();
$schedule->command('foo')->tuesdays();
$schedule->command('foo')->wednesdays();
// And so on
$schedule->command('foo')->weekdays();
```

If you have a potentially long-running command, then you can prevent it from overlapping:

```
$schedule->command('foo')->everyFiveMinutes()
        ->withoutOverlapping();
```

Along with the schedule, you can also specify the environment under which a scheduled command should run, as shown in the following command:

```
$schedule->command('foo')->weekly()->environments('production');
```

You could use this to run commands in a production environment, for example, archiving data or running a report periodically.

By default, scheduled commands won't execute if the maintenance mode is enabled. This behavior can be easily overridden:

```
$schedule->command('foo')->weekly()->evenInMaintenanceMode();
```

Viewing the output of scheduled commands

For some scheduled commands, you probably want to view the output somehow, whether that is via e-mail, logged to a file on disk, or sending a callback to a pre-defined URL. All of these scenarios are possible in Laravel.

To send the output of a job via e-mail by using the following command:

```
$schedule->command('foo')->weekly()
        ->emailOutputTo('someone@example.com');
```

If you wish to write the output of a job to a file on disk, that is easy enough too:

```
$schedule->command('foo')->weekly()->sendOutputTo($filepath);
```

You can also ping a URL after a job is run:

```
$schedule->command('foo')->weekly()->thenPing($url);
```

This will execute a GET request to the specified URL, at which point you could send a message to your favorite chat client to notify you that the command has run.

Finally, you can chain the preceding command to send multiple notifications:

```
$schedule->command('foo')->weekly()
        ->sendOutputTo($filepath)
        ->emailOutputTo('someone@example.com');
```

However, note that you have to send the output to a file before it can be e-mailed if you wish to do both.

Summary

In this chapter, you have learned the different ways in which Artisan can assist you in the development, debugging, and deployment process. We have also seen how easy it is to build a custom Artisan command and adapt it to your own needs.

If you are relatively new to the command line, you will have had a glimpse into the power of command-line utilities. If, on the other hand, you are a seasoned user of the command line and you have written scripts with other programming languages, you can surely appreciate the simplicity and expressiveness of Artisan.

In the next chapter, we will take a look at the features Laravel offers us to secure our application, as well as authenticating and authorizing users.

Authentication and Security

7

In this chapter, we will improve the application we built in *Chapter 3, Your First Application*, by adding a simple authentication mechanism and addressing any security issues with the existing code base. In doing so, you will learn about:

- Configuring and using the authentication service
- Middleware and how to apply it to specific routes
- Data validation and form requests
- The most common security vulnerabilities in web applications
- How Laravel can help you write more secure code

Authenticating users

Allowing users to register and sign in is an extremely common feature in web applications. Yet, PHP does not dictate how it should be done, nor does it give you any helpers to implement it. This has led to the creation of disparate, and sometimes insecure, methods of authenticating users and restricting access to specific pages. In that respect, Laravel provides you with different tools to make these features more secure and easier to integrate. It does so with the help of its authentication service and functionality that we have not covered yet — **middleware**.

Creating the user model

First of all, we need to define the model that will be used to represent the users of our application. Laravel already provides you with sensible defaults inside `config/auth.php`, where you can change the model or table that is used to store your user accounts.

It also comes with an existing `User` model inside `app/User.php`. For the purposes of this application, we are going to simplify it slightly, remove certain class variables, and add new methods so that it can interact with the `Cat` model as follows:

```php
namespace App;

use Illuminate\Auth\Authenticatable;
use Illuminate\Database\Eloquent\Model;
use Illuminate\Auth\Passwords\CanResetPassword;
use Illuminate\Contracts\Auth\Authenticatable
  as uthenticableContract;
use Illumunate\Contracts\Auth\CanResetPassword
  as CanResetPasswordContract;
use App\Cat;

class User extends Model implements AuthenticatableContract,
  CanResetPasswordContract {
  use Authenticable, CanResetPassword;
  public function cats() {
    return $this->hasMany('App\Cat');
  }
  public function owns(Cat $cat) {
    return $this->id == $cat->user_id;
  }
  public function canEdit(Cat $cat) {
    return $this->is_admin || $this->owns($cat);
  }
}
```

The first thing to note is that this model implements the `Authenticable` interface. Remember that an interface does not give any implementation details. It is nothing more than a **contract** that specifies the names of the methods that a class should define when it implements the interface. In this case, the `Authenticable` interface mandates that the following methods be implemented:

- `getAuthIdentifier`
- `getAuthPassword`
- `getRememberToken`
- `setRememberToken`
- `getRememberTokenName`

If you open the `app/User.php` file, you might wonder where these methods are. These methods are actually provided by the `Authenticable` trait. You can see the trait being included after the `User` class's opening brace:

```php
use Authenticable, CanResetPassword;
```

Traits allow the reuse of code within classes. This is to make up for a shortcoming of the PHP language, which does not allow **multiple inheritance** in classes. So, as a workaround, you can compose methods that may be dropped into multiple classes that might already be extending another base class.

In our User model, the cats() method simply defines the hasMany relationship with the Cat model. The last two methods will be used to check whether a given Cat instance is owned or is editable by the current User instance.

Finally, let's create a helper method on the User model that will allow us to check whether we have an administrator or not. This method will be suitably named isAdministrator as shown here:

```
public function isAdministrator()
{
  return $this->getAttribute('is_admin');
}
```

If using MySQL, this will return a string of either 0 or 1 (as MySQL doesn't have a native Boolean data type). We can, however, cast this model attribute to be a Boolean to make value checking a bit better. At the top of your model, add the following code:

```
protected $casts = [
  'is_admin' => 'boolean',
];
```

In this array, we define the attribute and what data type we actually want. Then, when we retrieve an attribute from the model, it will be cast to the specified data type.

Other data types that model attributes can be cast to are as follows:

* string
* integer
* real
* float
* double
* array

The array type can be used for columns that contain a serialized JSON string, which will de-serialize the data and present it as a plain PHP array.

The is_admin attribute doesn't exist in our users table currently, so let's fix that.

Creating the necessary database schema

As well as a `User` model, Laravel also comes pre-packaged with two migration files: one for creating the `users` table and the other to create the `password_resets` table.

By default, the user's table migration creates a table with columns for each user's ID, name, password, remember token, as well as the created at and updated at timestamps. We need to extend that table by adding a new column designating whether each user is an administrator of our application or not.

To do this, we can create another migration. Migrations can be used to alter existing tables as well as creating entirely new ones. In this instance, we're going to create a migration to add a Boolean column named `is_admin` to the `users` table.

Run the following command to create the migration file in `database/migrations`:

```
$ php artisan make:migration add_is_admin_column_to_users
```

Then change the `up` method as follows to contain the schema change:

```
public function up() {
  Schema::table('users', function(Blueprint $table) {
    $table->boolean('is_admin')->default(false)
      ->after('password');
  }
}
```

We set the default value to `false` so that we have to explicitly set it to `true` for any users we want to be administrators, rather than every new user (and any existing users in the database table) automatically being granted administrator privileges on creation.

As with any other migration, we also have to provide the `down` method to revert any changes. As we've created a column, we need to remove it if a user decides to roll back the migration:

```
public function down() {
  Schema::table('users', function(Blueprint $table) {
    $table->dropColumn('is_admin');
  });
}
```

Now, we also need to update the `cats` database table to add a column associating it with a user. By following the preceding steps, we create a new schema, as follows, describing the change:

```
$ php artisan make:migration add_user_id_column_to_cats
```

We then complete the methods as follows:

```
public function up() {
  Schema::table('cats', function(Blueprint $table) {
    $table->integer('user_id')->unsigned();
    $table->foreign('user_id')->references('id')->on('users')
      ->onDelete('cascade');
  });
}
```

With the preceding code, we alter the cats table to have a user_id column that stores the id of the Cat owner. After creating the column, we create a **foreign key constraint** on the table so that a user_id value has to match the primary key of a record in the users table. Foreign keys help you to enforce the consistency of data (for example, you will not be able to assign Cat to a nonexistent user). Cascading deletes also means that when a user is deleted, their associated cat records will be deleted too; otherwise, the database will end up containing cats that no longer have any owners!

The code to reverse this migration will simply remove the foreign key constraint and the column and then drop the user_id column:

```
public function down() {
  Schema::table('cats', function(Blueprint $table) {
    $table->dropForeign('cats_user_id_foreign');
    $table->dropColumn('user_id');
  });
}
```

Next, we prepare a database seeder to create two users for our application, one of which will be an administrator.

```
Use App\User;

class UsersTableSeeder extends Seeder {
  public function run() {
    User::create([
      'username' =>'admin',
      'password' => bcrypt('hunter2'),
      'is_admin' => true,
    ]);

    User::create([
      'username' => 'scott',
      'password' => bcrypt('tiger'),
      'is_admin' => false,
    ]);
  }
}
```

Once you have saved this code inside a new file named `database/seeds/`
`UsersTableSeeder.php`, do not forget to call it inside the main `DatabaseSeeder` class.

 Laravel expects all passwords to be hashed with the `bcrypt`
helper, which uses the **Bcrypt** algorithm to create a strong
hash. You should never store passwords in *cleartext* or hash
them with weak algorithms, such as `md5` or `sha1`.

To run the migration and seed the database at the same time, enter the
following command:

```
$ php artisan migrate --seed
```

Authentication routes and views

We have mentioned earlier that PHP has no standard way to authenticate users, but
this is not true of Laravel. Laravel realizes that the most modern web applications will
require users to register and log in, so it comes with controllers, routes, and views
to facilitate this from the get-go. You can find the main authentication controller at
`app/Http/Controllers/Auth/AuthController.php`. If you open the file, you will
see that all it contains is a constructor because like the `User` model, it uses a trait to
provide functionality, in this case, `AuthenticatesAndRegistersUsers`:

```
namespace App\Http\Controllers\Auth;

use App\Http\Controllers\Controller;
use Illuminate\Contracts\Auth\Guard;
use Illuminate\Contracts\Auth\Registrar;
use Illuminate\Foundation\Auth\AuthenticatesAndRegistersUsers;

class AuthController extends Controller {

  use AuthenticatesAndRegistersUsers;

  public function __construct(Guard $auth, Registrar $registrar) {
    $this->auth = $auth;
    $this->registrar = $registrar;

    $this->middleware('guest', ['except' => 'getLogout']);
  }
}
```

The `middleware` method will apply the guest middleware to all actions in the controller, except the `getLogout()` action. We'll look at middleware in more depth later in this chapter.

This controller (as well as the controller used for handling password resets) can be found in the application's routes file:

```
$router->controllers([
    'auth' => 'Auth\AuthController',
    'password' => 'Auth\PasswordController',
]);
```

Laravel also includes two views, `login.blade.php` and `register.blade.php`, at `resources/views/auth`.

Let's look at integrating Laravel's `auth` views into our application. We will start by amending our master layout (`resources/views/layouts/master.blade.php`) to display the login link to guests and the logout link to users who are logged in. To check whether a visitor is logged in, we use the `Auth::check()` method:

```
<div class="container">
  <div class="page-header">
    <div class="text-right">
      @if (Auth::check())
        Logged in as
        <strong>{{ Auth::user()->username }}</strong>
        {!! link_to('auth/logout', 'Log Out') !!}
      @else
        {!! link_to('auth/login', 'Log In') !!}
      @endif
    </div>
  @yield('header')
  </div>
  @if (Session::has('message'))
    <div class="alert alert-success">
      {{ Session::get('message') }}
    </div>
  @endif

  @if (Session::has('error'))
    <div class="alert alert-warning">
      {{ Session::get('error') }}
    </div>
  @endif
  @yield('content')
</div>
```

We can replace the login view, inside `resources/views/auth/login.blade.php`, with a simpler form:

```
@extends('layouts.master')
@section('header')<h2>Log In</h2>@stop
@section('main')
  {!! Form::open(['url' => 'auth/login']) !!}
  <div class="form-group">
    {!! Form::label('username', 'Username', ['class' =>
      'control-label']) !!}
    <div class="form-controls">
      {!! Form::text('username', null, ['class' =>
        'form-control']) !!}
    </div>
  </div>
  <div class="form-group">
    {!! Form::label('Password') !!}
    <div class="form-controls">
      {!! Form::password('password', ['class' =>
      'form-control']) !!}
    </div>
  </div>
  {!! Form::submit('Log in', ['class' => 'btn btn-primary']) !!}
  {!! Form::close() !!}
@stop
```

We use the Blade syntax to get the raw value (`{!! $value !!}`) from the HTML and Form helpers because they return HTML mark-up, and if we were to use the default syntax (`{{ $value }}`) to render these, we'd instead get the HTML string printed to the screen.

Middleware

If you refer back to the `AuthController`, you will notice the following line in the constructor method:

```
$this->middleware('auth', ['except' => 'getLogout']);
```

Middleware includes classes that can be attached to requests coming into your application, and used to alter the results of those requests. Middleware are a replacement for **route filters** that were found in Laravel 4.

Middleware can be registered either when defining routes, or in controllers as mentioned earlier. The preceding example attaches the `auth` middleware to all requests that will be handled by the `AuthController`, except for requests to the `getLogout` method.

Middleware classes can be found in the `app/Http/Middleware` directory. In here, you can find the default `Authentication` middleware class, as well as two others: `RedirectIfAuthenticated`, and `VerifyCsrfToken`. We can inspect the `Authentication` class to see how a middleware class works:

```php
public function __construct(Guard $auth) {
  $this->auth = $auth;
}

public function handle($request, Closure $next) {
  if ($this->auth->guest()) {
    if ($request->ajax()) {
      return response('Unauthorized', 401);
    } else {
      return redirect()->guest('auth/login');
    }
  }
  return $next($request);
}
```

There are two methods: the `constructor` and the `handle` methods. In the preceding example, the class is checking whether the current user is authenticated (using the `guest()` method on the `Guard` class) and if they are a guest, returning a response if the request was made via AJAX, or redirecting the user to the login form. Because the response is returned then and there, the request will not be processed any further.

We can use this approach to not only check if users have authenticated, but also to check whether they are administrators. We can use the in-built Artisan generator to create a new middleware class as follows:

$ php artisan make:middleware IsAdministrator

This will create a new file at `app/Http/Middleware/IsAdministrator.php`. Like the `Authentication` class, we need the `Guard` implementation, so add a constructor that type-hints the dependency so that the service container automatically injects it:

```php
public function __construct(Guard $auth) {
  $this->auth = $auth;
}
```

We'll also need to import the full namespace at the top of the file as follows:

```php
use Illuminate\Contracts\Auth\Guard;
```

Now we have a `Guard` instance and we assign it to a class property; we can now flesh out the `handle` method as follows:

```
public function handle($request, \Closure $next) {
  if ( ! $this->auth->user()->isAdministrator()) {
    if ($this->request->ajax()) {
      return response('Forbidden.', 403);
    } else {
      throw new AccessDeniedHttpException;
    }
  }
}
```

This time, we get the current user from the `Guard` (which will yield a `User` Eloquent model instance). We can then call any methods on this model. In the preceding example, we call our `isAdministrator()` method, which will return a Boolean value as to whether the user should be treated as an administrator or not. If not—like the `Authenticated` class—we return a simple string response (and the appropriate HTTP status code) if the request was made via AJAX; otherwise, we throw an `AccessDeniedHttpException`. This exception is actually part of the Symfony `HttpKernel` library, so we need to import the class's full namespace at the top of the file:

```
use Symfony\Component\HttpKernel\Exception\
  AccessDeniedHttpException;
```

The final step in creating a middleware is to tell the HTTP `Kernel` class about it. You can find this file at `app/Http/Kernel.php`. By opening the file, you will see two properties defined: `$middleware` and `$routeMiddleware`. Adding the class's full namespace to the `$middleware` array would add the middleware to every request. We don't want to do this because if we did, no one would be able to access the login page as they'd be unauthenticated at this point! Instead, we want to add an entry to the `$routeMiddleware` array as follows:

```
protected $routeMiddleware = [
  'auth' => 'App\Core\Http\Middleware\Authenticate',
  'auth.basic' =>
    Illuminate\Auth\Middleware\AuthenticateWithBasicAuth',
  'guest' =>
    'App\Core\Http\Middleware\RedirectIfAuthenticated',
  'admin' => 'App\Http\Middleware\IsAdministrator',
];
```

The key in the array is what we can then use on routes and in controllers, and the corresponding class will be applied when requesting the specified resource.

The following is an example applying it to a route:

```
Route::get('admin/dashboard', [
  'middleware' => ['auth', 'admin'],
  'uses' => '\Admin\DashboardController@index',
]);
```

As you can see, you can specify multiple middleware classes to apply to a single request. In the previous route example, first the Authenticated middleware class will be called; if all is good (and the user wasn't redirected to the login page), it will then be passed to the IsAdministrator middleware class, which will check whether the currently logged in user is an administrator.

Validating user input

Our application still has a major flaw—it does not perform any validation on the data submitted by users. While you might end up with a series of conditions with regular expressions here and there if you were to do this in plain PHP, Laravel offers a far more straightforward and robust way to achieve this.

Validation is performed by passing an array with the input data and an array with the validation rules to the Validator::make($data, $rules) method. In the case of our application, here are the rules we could write:

```
$rules = [
  'name' => 'required|min:3', // Required, > 3 characters
  'date_of_birth' => ['required, 'date'] // Must be a date
];
```

Multiple validation rules can be separated by either pipes or passed as an array (examples of both are shown in the preceding code). Laravel provides over 30 different validation rules, and they are all documented in here:

http://laravel.com/docs/validation#available-validation-rules

Here is how we will check these rules with the data submitted in the form:

```
$validator = Validator::make($rules, Input::all());
```

You can then make your application act based on the output of `$validator->fails()`. If this method call returns `true`, you will retrieve an object containing all error messages with `$validator->messages()`. If you were validating data in a controller action, you could attach this object to a redirection that sends the user back to the form:

```
return redirect()
  ->back()
  ->with('errors, $validatior->messages());
```

Since each field can have zero or more validation errors, you will use a condition and a loop with the following methods to display those messages:

```
if ($errors->has('name')) {
  foreach ($errors->get('name') as $error) {
    echo $error;
  }
}
```

You might also use a tool such as Ardent, which extends Eloquent and lets you to write validation rules directly inside the model. You can download Ardent from the following link:

```
https://github.com/laravelbook/ardent
```

Form requests

In Laravel 4, you were free to place validation anywhere you wanted. This led to developers implementing validation in a myriad of ways, including in the controller or as a validation service. In version 5, Laravel introduced a way of standardizing how validation was performed on submitted data, via **form requests**.

Form requests are classes that wrap the standard `Request` class in Laravel, but implements a trait named `ValidatesWhenResolved`. This trait contains a `Validator` instance, and uses rules you define in your form request class to validate the data in the request. If the validator passes, then the controller action it was applied to will be executed as normal. If the validator fails, then the user is redirected to the previous URL with the errors in the session. This means you don't need to define validation routines in your controller actions, and you can even re-use them across controller actions where the same data can be submitted but in different scenarios.

Let's create a form request for saving a cat's details. Again, Artisan comes with a generator to create a new form request class for us:

```
$ php artisan make:request SaveCatRequest
```

This will create the file at `app/Http/Requests/SaveCatRequest.php`. Inside the file, you will find two methods: `authorize` and `rules`.

Before validation is performed, the form request authorizes the current request. The implementation detail is up to you. You might want the current user to be logged in, or to be an administrator. You can define that logic in this method. By default, it simply returns `false`. This isn't ideal as it means *no one* would be able to perform this request. Since we're handling user authentication via middleware, we can simply switch this to return `true` instead.

The second method, `rules`, is where we supply the array of validation rules to be fed to the `Validator` instance. Taking the preceding `Validator` example, this can be changed to the following code:

```
public function rules() {
  return [
    'name' => 'required|min:3',
    'date_of_birth' => 'required|date',
  ];
}
```

The reason rules are defined in a method and not simply as a class property is to allow for conditional validation. There may be times when you only want to validate a certain field, for example, if a value is provided in another field. Imagine a checkout form in an e-commerce website that asks a user for a billing address and an optional shipping address if it's different from the billing address. Most online stores will have a checkbox that when checked, will display the fields to enter the shipping address. If we were to create the validation for this scenario, then it may look something like the following code:

```
public function rules() {
  $rules = [
    'billing_address' => 'required',
  ];
  if ($request->has('shipping_address_different')) {
    $rules['shipping_address'] = 'required';
  }
  return $rules;
}
```

The preceding example checks whether a field with `shipping_address_different` (the checkbox) is present and, if so, appends a validation rule to specify that `shipping_address` is required. As you can see, this makes validation in form requests very powerful.

Form request classes are instantiated by specifying them as a parameter to the controller action you want them to apply. In our case of saving cats, this will apply to both the `create` and `update` methods in our `CatsController` class:

```
public function create(SaveCatRequest $request) {
  // method body
}

public function update(SaveCatRequest $request) {
  // method body
}
```

Now, whenever either of these actions is requested, the `SaveCatRequest` class will first be called and checked to see whether the data is valid. This means our controller methods can stay lean, and only deal with the actual persisting of the new data to the database.

Securing your application

Before you deploy your application in a hostile environment, full of merciless bots and malicious users, there are a number of security considerations that you must keep in mind. In this section, we are going to cover several common attack vectors for web applications and learn about how Laravel protects your application against them. Since a framework cannot protect you against everything, we will also look at the common pitfalls to avoid.

Cross-site request forgery

Cross-site request forgery (**CSRF**) attacks are conducted by targeting a URL that has side effects (that is, it is performing an action and not just displaying information). We have already partly mitigated CSRF attacks by avoiding the use of GET for routes that have permanent effects such as DELETE/cats/1, since it is not reachable from a simple link or embeddable in an `<iframe>` element. However, if an attacker is able to send his victim to a page that he controls, he can easily make the victim submit a form to the target domain. If the victim is already logged in on the target domain, the application would have no way of verifying the authenticity of the request.

The most efficient countermeasure is to issue a token whenever a form is displayed and then check that token when the form is submitted. `Form::open` and `Form::model` both automatically insert a hidden _token input element, and middleware is applied to check the supplied token on incoming requests to see whether it matches the expected value.

Escaping content to prevent cross-site scripting (XSS)

Cross-site scripting (**XSS**) attacks happen when attackers are able to place client-side JavaScript code in a page viewed by other users. In our application, assuming that the name of our cat is not escaped, if we enter the following snippet of code as the value for the name, every visitor will be greeted with an alert message everywhere the name of our cat is displayed:

```
Evil Cat <script>alert('Meow!')</script>
```

While this is a rather harmless script, it would be very easy to insert a longer script or link to an external script that steals the session or cookie values. To avoid this kind of attack, you should never trust any user-submitted data or escape any dangerous characters. You should favor the double-brace syntax ({{ $value }}) in your Blade templates, and only use the {!! $value !!} syntax, where you're certain the data is safe to display in its raw format.

Avoiding SQL injection

An **SQL injection** vulnerability exists when an application inserts arbitrary and unfiltered user input in an SQL query. This user input can come from cookies, server variables, or, most frequently, through GET or POST input values. These attacks are conducted to access or modify data that is not normally available and sometimes to disturb the normal functioning of the application.

By default, Laravel will protect you against this type of attack since both the query builder and Eloquent use **PHP Data Objects** (**PDO**) class behind the scenes. PDO uses **prepared statements**, which allows you to safely pass any parameters without having to escape and sanitize them.

In some cases, you might want to write more complex or database-specific queries in SQL. This is possible using the DB::raw method. When using this method, you must be very careful not to create any vulnerable queries like the following one:

```
Route::get('sql-injection-vulnerable', function() {
  $name = "'Bobby' OR 1=1";
  return DB::select(
    DB::raw("SELECT * FROM cats WHERE name = $name"));
});
```

To protect this query from SQL injection, you need to rewrite it by replacing the parameters with question marks in the query and then pass the values in an array as a second argument to the `raw` method:

```
Route::get('sql-injection-not-vulnerable', function() {
    $name = "'Bobby' OR 1=1";
    return DB::select(
        DB::raw("SELECT * FROM cats WHERE name = ?", [$name]));
});
```

The preceding query is known as a **prepared statement**, as we define the query and what parameters are expected, and any harmful parameters that would alter the query or data in the database in an unintended way are sanitized.

Using mass assignment with care

In *Chapter 3, Your First Application*, we used mass assignment, a convenient feature that allows us to create a model based on the form input without having to assign each value individually.

This feature should, however, be used carefully. A malicious user could alter the form on the client side and add a new input to it:

```
<input name="is_admin" value="1" />
```

Then, when the form is submitted, we attempt to create a new model using the following code:

```
Cat::create(Request::all())
```

Thanks to the `$fillable` array, which defines a white list of fields that can be filled through mass assignment, this method call will throw a mass assignment exception.

It is also possible to do the opposite and define a blacklist with the `$guarded` property. However, this option can be potentially dangerous since you might forget to update it when adding new fields to the model.

Cookies – secure by default

Laravel makes it very easy to create, read, and expire cookies with its `Cookie` class.

You will also be pleased to know that all cookies are automatically signed and encrypted. This means that if they are tampered with, Laravel will automatically discard them. This also means that you will not be able to read them from the client side using JavaScript.

Forcing HTTPS when exchanging sensitive data

If you are serving your application over HTTP, you need to bear in mind that every bit of information that is exchanged, including passwords, is sent in *cleartext*. An attacker on the same network could therefore intercept private information, such as session variables, and log in as the victim. The only way we can prevent this is to use HTTPS. If you already have an SSL certificate installed on your web server, Laravel comes with a number of helpers to switch between `http://` and `https://` and restrict access to certain routes. You can, for instance, define an `https` filter that will redirect the visitor to the secure route as shown in the following code snippet:

```
Route::filter('https', function() {
  if ( ! Request::secure())
    return Redirect::secure(URI::current());
});
```

Summary

In this chapter, we learned how to make use of many of Laravel's tools to add authentication features to a website, validate data, and avoid common security problems. You should now have all the necessary information to create a Laravel application, test them, and secure them.

In the *Appendix*, *An Arsenal of Tools*, you will be presented with a handy reference for many of the other helpful features that Laravel offers out of the box.

An Arsenal of Tools

Laravel comes with several utilities that help you perform specific tasks, such as sending e-mails, queuing functions, and manipulating files. It ships with a ton of handy utilities that it uses internally; the good news is that you can also use them in your applications. This chapter will present the most useful utilities so you do not end up rewriting a function that already exists in the framework!

The structure of this chapter is partly based on *Jesse O'Brien's* cheat sheet, which is accessible at `http://cheats.jesse-obrien.ca/`. The examples are based on Laravel's tests as well as its official documentation and API.

Array helpers

Arrays are the bread and butter of any web application that deals with data. PHP already offers nearly 80 functions to perform various operations on arrays, and Laravel complements them with a handful of practical functions that are inspired by certain functions found in Python and Ruby.

> Several of Laravel's classes, including Eloquent collections, implement the PHP `ArrayAccess` interface. This means that you can use them like a normal array in your code and, for instance, iterate over the items in a `foreach` loop or use them with the array functions described here.

Most of the functions support a **dot notation** to refer to nested values, which is similar to JavaScript objects. For example, rather than writing `$arr['foo']['bar']['baz']`, you can use the `array_get` helper and write `array_get($arr, 'foo.bar.baz');`.

In the following usage examples, we will use three dummy arrays and assume that they are reset for each example:

```
$associative = [
    'foo' => 1,
    'bar' => 2,
];
$multidimensional = [
    'foo' => [
        'bar' => 123,
    ],
];
$list_key_values = [
    ['foo' => 'bar'],
    ['foo' => 'baz'],
];
```

The usage examples of array helpers

We will now take a look at how we can use Laravel's array helper functions to extract and manipulate the values of those arrays:

- To retrieve a value with a fallback value if the key does not exist, we use the `array_get` function as follows:

  ```
  array_get($multidimensional, 'foo.bar', 'default');
  // Returns 123
  ```

  This is helpful if you are referencing an array key that may or may not exist (that is, in an array of request data). If the key does not exist, then the default value will be returned instead.

- To remove a value from an array using the dot notation, we use the `array_forget` function as follows:

  ```
  array_forget($multidimensional, 'foo.bar');
  // $multidimensional == ['foo' => []];
  ```

- To remove a value from an array and return it, we use the `array_pull` function as follows:

  ```
  array_pull($multidimensional, 'foo.bar');
  // Returns 123 and removes the value from the array
  ```

- To set a nested value using the dot notation, we use the `array_set` function as follows:

  ```
  array_set($multidimensional, 'foo.baz', '456');
  // $multidimensional == ['foo' => ['bar' =>
     123, 'baz' => '456']];
  ```

- To flatten a multidimensional associative array, we use the `array_dot` function as follows:

```
array_dot($multidimensional);
// Returns ['foo.bar' => 123];
array_dot($list_key_values);
// Returns ['0.foo' => 'bar', '1.foo' => 'baz'];
```

- To return all of the keys and their values from the array except for the ones that are specified, we use the `array_except` function as follows:

```
array_except($associative, ['foo']);
// Returns ['bar' => 2];
```

- To only extract some keys from an array, we use the `array_only` function as follows:

```
array_only($associative, ['bar']);
// Returns ['bar' => 2];
```

- To return a flattened array containing all of the nested values (the keys are dropped), we use the `array_fetch` function as follows:

```
array_fetch($list_key_values, 'foo');
// Returns ['bar', 'baz'];
```

- To iterate over the array and return the first value for which the closure returns true, we use the `array_first` function as follows:

```
array_first($associative, function($key, $value) {
    return $key == 'foo';
});
// Returns 1
```

- To generate a one-dimensional array containing only the values that are found in a multidimensional array, we use the `array_flatten` function as follows:

```
array_flatten($multidimensional);
// Returns [123]
```

- To extract an array of values from a list of key-value pairs, we use the `array_pluck` function as follows:

```
array_pluck($list_key_values, 'foo');
// Returns ['bar', 'baz'];
```

- To get the first or last item of an array (this also works with the values returned by functions), we use the `head` and `last` functions as follows:

```
head($array); // Aliases to reset($array)
last($array); // Aliases to end($array)
```

String and text manipulation

The string manipulation functions are found in the `Illuminate\Support` namespace and are callable on the `Str` object.

Most of the functions also have shorter `snake_case` aliases. For example, the `Str::endsWith()` method is identical to the global `ends_with()` function. We are free to use whichever one we prefer in our application.

Boolean functions

The following functions return the `true` or `false` values:

- The `is` method checks whether a value matches a pattern. The asterisk can be used as a wildcard character as shown here:

  ```
  Str::is('projects/*', 'projects/php/'); // Returns true
  ```

- The `contains` method, as shown in the following code, checks whether a string contains a given substring:

  ```
  Str::contains('Getting Started With Laravel', 'Python');
  // returns false
  ```

- The `startsWith` and `endsWith` methods, as shown in the following code, check whether a string starts or ends with one or more substrings:

  ```
  Str::startsWith('.gitignore', '.git'); // Returns true
  Str::endsWith('index.php', ['html', 'php']); //
    Returns true
  ```

As you can see from the preceding examples, these methods are handy for validation filenames and similar data.

Transformation functions

In some cases, you need to transform a string before displaying it to the user or using it in a URL. Laravel provides the following helpers to achieve this:

- This function generates a URL-friendly string:

  ```
  Str::slug('A/B testing is fun!');
  // Returns "ab-testing-is-fun"
  ```

- This function generates a title where every word is capitalized:

  ```
  Str::title('getting started with laravel');
  // Returns 'Getting Started With Laravel'
  ```

- This function caps a string with an instance of a given character:
```
Str::finish('/one/trailing/slash', '/');
Str::finish('/one/trailing/slash/', '/');
// Both will return '/one/trailing/slash/'
```

- This function limits the number of **characters** in a string:
```
Str::limit($value, $limit = 100, $end = '...')
```

- This function limits the number of **words** in a string:
```
Str::words($value, $words = 100, $end = '...')
```

Inflection functions

The following functions help you find out the plural or singular form of a word, even if it is irregular:

- This function finds out the plural form of a word:
```
Str::plural('cat');
// Returns 'cats'
Str::plural('fish');
// Returns 'fish'
Str::plural('monkey');
// Returns 'monkeys'
```

- This function finds out the singular form of a word:
```
Str::singular('elves');
// Returns 'elf'
```

Dealing with files

Laravel 5 includes the excellent **Flysystem** project for interacting with files both in the application filesystem, as well as popular cloud-based storage solutions such as **Amazon Simple Storage Service (Amazon S3)** and **Rackspace**. Filesystems are configured as *disks* in the config/filesystems.php file. You can then use a consistent API to manage files, whether they are located locally or in an external cloud store.

Calling methods directly on the Storage façade will call those methods on the default disk as follows:

```
Storage::exists('foo.txt');
```

You can also explicitly specify the disk to perform actions on, in case you have more than one disk configured, as follows:

```
Storage::disk('local')->exists('foo.txt');
```

You can read and write data to files as follows:

```
Storage::put('foo.txt', $contents);
$contents = Storage::get('foo.txt');
```

You can also prepend or append data instead as follows:

```
Storage::prepend('foo.txt', 'Text to prepend.');
Storage::append('foo.txt', 'Text to append.');
```

You can copy and move files with the aptly-named methods as follows:

```
Storage::copy($source, $destination);
Storage::move($source, $destination);
```

And you can also delete files, either one at a time or multiple files in one go, by supplying an array of files to delete, as shown in the following code:

```
Storage::delete('foo.txt');
Storage::delete(['foo.txt', 'bar.txt']);
```

There are also various other helpful methods that allow you to retrieve useful information about a file as follows:

```
Storage::size('foo.txt');
Storage::lastModified('foo.txt');
```

Apart from working with files, you can work with directories. To list all files within a particular directory use the following code:

```
Storage::files('path/to/directory');
```

The preceding code will only list files in the current directory. If you wanted to list all files recursively (that is, files in the current directory and any subdirectories), then you can use the `allFiles` method as follows:

```
Storage::allFiles('path/to/directory');
```

You can create directories as follows:

```
Storage::makeDirectory('path/to/directory');
```

And you can also delete directories as follows:

```
Storage::deleteDirectory('path/to/directory');
```

File uploads

Handling file uploads is easy in Laravel 5. The first step is to create a form that will send files when submitted:

```
{!! Form::open(['files' => true) !!}
```

This will set the `enctype` attribute to `multipart/form-data`. You then need an HTML `file` input:

```
{!! Form::file('avatar') !!}
```

On submission, you can access the file from the `Request` object in your controller actions as follows:

```
public function store(Request $request)
{
  $file = $request->file('avatar');
}
```

From here, you will normally move the file to a directory of your choice:

```
public function store(Request $request)
{
  $file = $request->file('avatar');
  $file->move(storage_path('uploads/avatars'));
}
```

In the preceding example, `$file` is an instance of the `Symfony\Component\HttpFoundation\File\UploadedFile` class, which provides a number of handy methods for interacting with the uploaded file.

You can get the full path to the file as follows:

```
$path = $request->file('avatar')->getRealPath();
```

You can get the name of the file as uploaded by the user as follows:

```
$name = $request->file('avatar')->getClientOriginalName();
```

You can also retrieve just the extension of the original file as follows:

```
$ext = $request->file('avatar')->getClientOriginalExtension();
```

Sending e-mails

Laravel's `Mail` class extends the popular Swift Mailer package, which makes sending e-mails a breeze. The e-mail templates are loaded in the same way as views, which means you can use the Blade syntax and inject data into your templates:

- To inject some data into a template located inside `resources/views/email/view.blade.php`, we use the following function:

  ```
  Mail::send('email.view', $data, function($message) {});
  ```

- To send both an HTML and a plain text version, we use the following function:

  ```
  Mail::send(array('html.view', 'text.view'), $data,
  $callback);
  ```

- To delay the e-mail by 5 minutes (this requires a queue), we use the following function:

  ```
  Mail::later(5, 'email.view', $data, function($message) {});
  ```

Inside the `$callback` closure that receives the message object, we can call the following methods to alter the message that is to be sent:

- `$message->subject('Welcome to the Jungle');`

- `$message->from('email@example.com', 'Mr. Example');`

- `$message->to('email@example.com', 'Mr. Example');`

Some of the less common methods include:

- `$message->sender('email@example.com', 'Mr. Example');`

- `$message->returnPath('email@example.com');`

- `$message->cc('email@example.com', 'Mr. Example');`

- `$message->bcc('email@example.com', 'Mr. Example');`

- `$message->replyTo('email@example.com', 'Mr. Example');`

- `$message->priority(2);`

To attach or embed files, you can use the following methods:

- `$message->attach('path/to/attachment.txt');`

- `$message->embed('path/to/attachment.jpg');`

If you already have the data in memory, and you do not want to create additional files, you can use either the `attachData` or the `embedData` method as follows:

- `$message->attachData($data, 'attachment.txt');`

- `$message->embedData($data, 'attachment.jpg');`

Embedding is generally done with image files, and you can use either the `embed` or the `embedData` method directly inside the body of a message, as shown in the following code snippet:

```
<p>Product Screenshot:</p>
<p>{!! $message->embed('screenshot.jpg') !!}</p>
```

Easier date and time handling with Carbon

Laravel bundles Carbon (`https://github.com/briannesbitt/Carbon`), which extends and augments PHP's native `DateTime` object with more expressive methods. Laravel uses it mainly to provide more expressive methods on the date and time properties (`created_at`, `updated_at`, and `deleted_at`) of an Eloquent object. However, since the library is already there, it would be a shame not to use it elsewhere in the code of your application.

Instantiating Carbon objects

Carbon objects are meant to be instantiated like normal `DateTime` objects. They do, however, support a handful of more expressive methods:

- Carbon objects can be instantiated using the default constructor that will use the current date and time as follows:

    ◦ `$now = new Carbon();`

- They can be instantiated using the current date and time in a given timezone as follows:

    ◦ `$jetzt = new Carbon('Europe/Berlin');`

- They can be instantiated using expressive methods as follows:

    ◦ `$yesterday = Carbon::yesterday();`
    ◦ `$demain = Carbon::tomorrow('Europe/Paris');`

- They can be instantiated using exact parameters as follows:
  - `Carbon::createFromDate($year, $month, $day, $tz);`
  - `Carbon::createFromTime($hour, $minute, $second, $tz);`
  - `Carbon::create($year, $month, $day, $hour, $minute, $second, $tz);`

Outputting user-friendly timestamps

We can generate human-readable, relative timestamps such as *5 minutes ago, last week,* or *in a year* with the `diffForHumans()` method as follows:

```
$post = App\Post::find(123);
echo $post->created_at->diffForHumans();
```

Boolean methods

Carbon also provides a handful of simple and expressive methods that will come in handy in your controllers and views:

- `$date->isWeekday();`
- `$date->isWeekend();`
- `$date->isYesterday();`
- `$date->isToday();`
- `$date->isTomorrow();`
- `$date->isFuture();`
- `$date->isPast();`
- `$date->isLeapYear();`

Carbon for Eloquent DateTime properties

To be able to call Carbon's methods on attributes stored as DATE or DATETIME types in the database, you need to list them in a `$dates` property in the model:

```
class Post extends Model {
  // ...
  protected $dates = [
    'published_at',
    'deleted_at',
  ];
}
```

You don't need to include created_at or updated_at, as these are automatically treated as dates.

Don't wait any longer with queues

Queues allow you to defer the execution of functions without blocking the script. They can be used to run all sorts of functions, from e-mailing a large number of users to generating PDF reports.

Laravel 5 is compatible with the following queue drivers:

- Beanstalkd, with the `pda/pheanstalk` package
- Amazon SQS, with the `aws/aws-sdk-php` package
- IronMQ, with the `iron-io/iron_mq` package

Each queue system has its advantages. Beanstalkd can be installed on your own server; Amazon SQS might be more cost-effective and require less maintenance, as will IronMQ, which is also cloud-based. The latter also lets you set up *push queues*, which are great if you cannot run background jobs on your server.

Creating a command and pushing it onto the queue

Jobs come in the form of commands. Commands can be either self-handling or not. In the latter case, a corresponding handler class would take the data from the command class and then act upon it.

Command classes reside in the `app/Commands` directory, and command handler classes can be found in the `app/Handlers/Commands` directory. Classes for a command and its handler can be generated with an Artisan command as follows:

```
$ php artisan make:command CommandName --handler --queued
```

The `--handler` option tells Artisan to create a handler class (omitting this option would create a self-handling command class only), and the `--queued` option designates that this should be added to the queue, instead of being handled synchronously.

You can then use the `Queue` façade to add the command to the queue:

```
Queue::push(new SendConfirmationEmail($order));
```

Alternatively, you can dispatch commands using the **command bus**. The command bus is set up by default in controllers using the `DispatchesCommands` trait. This means in your controller actions you could use the `dispatch` method:

```
public function purchase(Product $product)
{
```

```
   // Create order
   $this->dispatch(new SendConfirmationEmail($order));
}
```

Commands are simple classes that contain the data needed to execute an action — the handler then performs the actual processing at a later stage using the data provided by the command. An example may be sending a confirmation e-mail after an order is placed. The command for this will look like the following:

```php
<?php namespace App\Commands;

use App\Order;
use Illuminate\Contracts\Queue\ShouldBeQueued;
use Illuminate\Queue\InteractsBeQueued;
use Illuminate\Queue\SerializesModels;

class SendConfirmationEmail extends Command implements
  ShouldBeQueued {

  use InteractsWithQueue, SerializesModels;

  public $order;

  public function __construct(Order $order) {
    $this->order = $order;
  }
}
```

The handler — when executed by the queue — will then perform the actual sending of the e-mail, passing the order to the e-mail template to display the details of the customer's purchase as follows:

```php
<?php namespace App\Handlers\Commands;

use App\Commands\SendConfirmationEmail;
use Illuminate\Contracts\Mail\Mailer;
use Illuminate\Queue\InteractsWithQueue;

class SendConfirmationEmailHandler {

  public function __construct(Mailer $mail) {
    $this->mail = $mail;
  }

  public function handle(SendConfirmationEmail $command) {
    $order = $command->order;
    $data = compact('order');
    $this->mail->send('emails.order.confirmation', $data,
      function($message) use ($order) {
```

```
                $message->subject('Your order confirmation');
                $message->to(
                  $order->customer->email,
                  $order->customer->name
                );
          });
      }
}
```

As command handlers are resolved via the service container, we can type-hint dependencies. In the preceding case, we need the mailer service, so we type-hint the contract to get an implementation. We can then use the mailer to send an e-mail to the customer using the order data received from the command class.

> The app/Commands directory will be renamed app/Jobs from Laravel 5.1 to indicate it is primarily for queued jobs.

Listening to a queue and executing jobs

The following are the functions used for listening to a queue and executing jobs:

- We can listen to the default queue as follows:

  ```
  $ php artisan queue:listen
  ```

- We can specify the connection on which to listen as follows:

  ```
  $ php artisan queue:listen connection
  ```

- We can specify multiple connections in the order of their priority as follows:

  ```
  $ php artisan queue:listen important,not-so-important
  ```

The queue:listen command has to run in the background in order to process the jobs as they arrive from the queue. To make sure that it runs permanently, you have to use a process control system such as **forever** (https://github.com/nodejitsu/forever) or **supervisor** (http://supervisord.org/).

Getting notified when a job fails

To get notified when a job fails, we use the following functions and commands:

- The following event listener is used for finding the failed jobs:

  ```
  Queue::failing(function($job, $data) {
    // Send email notification
  });
  ```

- Any of the failed jobs can be stored in a database table and viewed with the following commands:

```
$ php artisan queue:failed-table // Create the table
$ php artisan queue:failed // View the failed jobs
```

Queues without background processes

Push queues do not require a background process but they only work with the `iron.io` driver. Push queues will call an endpoint in your application when a job is received, rather than to a queue that is handled by a constantly-running worker process. This is handy if you do not have the ability to define the processes, which run on your application's server (such as is the case on shared hosting packages). After signing up for an account on `iron.io` and adding your credentials to `app/config/queue.php`, you use them by defining a `POST` route that receives all the incoming jobs. This route calls `Queue::marshal()`, which is the method responsible for firing the correct job handler:

```
Route::post('queue/receive', function() {
    return Queue::marshal();
});
```

This route then needs to be registered as a subscriber with the `queue:subscribe` command:

```
$ php artisan queue:subscribe queue_name
    http://yourapp.example.com/queue/receive
```

Once the URL is subscribed on `http://iron.io/`, any newly created jobs with `Queue::push()` will be sent from Iron back to your application via a `POST` request.

Where to go next?

The following is a list of the resources and sites that you can visit to keep up with the latest changes in Laravel:

- `http://twitter.com/laravelphp` on Twitter for regular updates
- `http://laravel.com/docs` for the complete documentation
- `http://laravel.com/api` for the browsable API
- `http://laracasts.com` for screencast tutorials

Index

S

Silex 43
Slim 43
SQL injection
  avoiding 101
string manipulation 108

T

testing
  benefits 66
tests
  anatomy 66, 67
  benefits 66
  tasks 66
text manipulation 108
transformation functions 108

U

unit testing
  assertions 68, 69
  exceptions, expecting 69
  interdependent classes in isolation,
      testing 70
  objects, cleaning up 69
  scene, preparing 69
  with PHPUnit 68
user input, validating
  form requests 98, 99
users, authenticating
  about 87
  database schema, creating 90-92
  middleware 94-96
  routes, authenticating 92-94
  user input, validating 97, 98
  user model, creating 87-89
  views, authenticating 92-94

V

Vagrant
  URL 18
validation rules
  URL 97
view composers 40
views
  authenticating 92-94
  returning 28
VirtualBox
  URL 17
Virtual Machines (VMs) 17

W

WampServer 17

Thank you for buying
Laravel 5 Essentials

About Packt Publishing

Packt, pronounced 'packed', published its first book, *Mastering phpMyAdmin for Effective MySQL Management*, in April 2004, and subsequently continued to specialize in publishing highly focused books on specific technologies and solutions.

Our books and publications share the experiences of your fellow IT professionals in adapting and customizing today's systems, applications, and frameworks. Our solution-based books give you the knowledge and power to customize the software and technologies you're using to get the job done. Packt books are more specific and less general than the IT books you have seen in the past. Our unique business model allows us to bring you more focused information, giving you more of what you need to know, and less of what you don't.

Packt is a modern yet unique publishing company that focuses on producing quality, cutting-edge books for communities of developers, administrators, and newbies alike. For more information, please visit our website at www.packtpub.com.

About Packt Open Source

In 2010, Packt launched two new brands, Packt Open Source and Packt Enterprise, in order to continue its focus on specialization. This book is part of the Packt Open Source brand, home to books published on software built around open source licenses, and offering information to anybody from advanced developers to budding web designers. The Open Source brand also runs Packt's Open Source Royalty Scheme, by which Packt gives a royalty to each open source project about whose software a book is sold.

Writing for Packt

We welcome all inquiries from people who are interested in authoring. Book proposals should be sent to author@packtpub.com. If your book idea is still at an early stage and you would like to discuss it first before writing a formal book proposal, then please contact us; one of our commissioning editors will get in touch with you.

We're not just looking for published authors; if you have strong technical skills but no writing experience, our experienced editors can help you develop a writing career, or simply get some additional reward for your expertise.

Getting Started with Laravel 4

ISBN: 978-1-78328-703-1   Paperback: 128 pages

Discover Laravel – one of the most expressive, robust, and flexible PHP web application frameworks around

1. Provides a concise introduction to all the concepts needed to get started with Laravel.

2. Walks through the different steps involved in creating a complete Laravel application.

3. Gives an overview of Laravel's advanced features that can be used when applications grow in complexity.

4. Learn how to build structured, more maintainable, and more secure applications with less code by using Laravel.

Learning Laravel 4 Application Development

ISBN: 978-1-78328-057-5   Paperback: 256 pages

Develop real-world web applications in Laravel 4 using its refined and expressive syntax

1. Build real-world web applications using the Laravel 4 framework.

2. Learn how to configure, optimize and deploy Laravel 4 applications.

3. Packed with illustrations along with lots of tips and tricks to help you learn more about one of the most exciting PHP frameworks around.

Please check **www.PacktPub.com** for information on our titles

Laravel Starter

ISBN: 978-1-78216-090-8   Paperback: 64 pages

The definitive introduction to the Laravel PHP web development framework

1. Learn something new in an Instant! A short, fast, focused guide delivering immediate results.

2. Create databases using Laravel's migrations.

3. Learn how to implement powerful relationships with Laravel's own "Eloquent" ActiveRecord implementation.

4. Learn about maximizing code reuse with the bundles.

Laravel Application Development Cookbook

ISBN: 978-1-78216-282-7   Paperback: 272 pages

Over 90 recipes to learn all the key aspects of Laravel, including installation, authentication, testing, and the deployment and integration of third parties in your application

1. Install and set up a Laravel application and then deploy and integrate third parties in your application.

2. Create a secure authentication system and build a RESTful API.

3. Build your own Composer Package and incorporate JavaScript and AJAX methods into Laravel.